The Theory and Practice
of Pension Funding

The Theory and Practice of Pension Funding

C. L. Trowbridge, F.S.A., M.A.A.A.
Senior Vice President and Chief Actuary
Bankers Life Company

C. E. Farr, F.S.A., M.A.A.A.
Second Vice President and Actuary
Bankers Life Company

 1976

RICHARD D. IRWIN, INC. Homewood, Illinois 60430
Irwin-Dorsey Limited Georgetown, Ontario L7G 4B3

First Printing, July 1976

ISBN 0-256-01881-2
Library of Congress Catalog Card No. 76–17351
Printed in the United States of America

Foreword
For the Society of Actuaries

IT IS A PRIVILEGE to acknowledge, with thanks, the efforts of C. L. Trowbridge and C. E. Farr in producing an important book on the actuarial aspects of pension funding.

This work is a part of the Society of Actuaries' continuing program for sustaining and enlarging the literature of actuarial science. The genesis of this effort can be traced to 1974, when chairmen of two Society of Actuaries pension committees gave voice to the serious gap in the actuarial literature of pensions. With the encouragement of then-President Edward Lew, the two authors volunteered to fill the void. The Trowbridge-Farr text is the happy result.

The Society of Actuaries is pleased to have arranged for the publication of this book. Although this work was written for a broad audience, it has already been adopted by the Education and Examination Committee as part of the Society's course of reading for actuarial students. It is best viewed as a general text on pension funding, useful to the experienced pension actuary as well as to advanced students seeking an introduction to the topic.

As the authors make clear in the Preface, the statements made and the views expressed are theirs alone, and are not those of the Society of Actuaries. With this understanding, the Society of Actuaries is pleased to sponsor *The Theory and Practice of Pension Funding*.

June 1976

JOHN M. BRAGG
President
Society of Actuaries

Foreword
For the American Academy of Actuaries

C. L. Trowbridge and C. E. Farr have produced a book which is a valuable addition to the actuarial literature on pensions. The book, a modern treatment of actuarial aspects of pension funding, includes material current with the passage of the Employee Retirement Income Security Act of 1974 (ERISA).

ERISA created a classification of individuals known as "enrolled actuaries," who are to provide actuarial certifications under the Act. The certifications by enrolled actuaries are a significant cornerstone in assuring the sound financing of pension plans.

This book was written with this audience specifically in mind, and will be a valuable reference for enrolled actuaries to use in professionally discharging their duties and responsibilities under the law. It will also serve as a valuable textbook for those individuals aspiring to become enrolled actuaries.

The American Academy of Actuaries, through its Committee on Services to Enrolled Actuaries, is pleased to endorse *The Theory and Practice of Pension Funding* as part of its program of services to enrolled actuaries, with the understanding that the statements made and the views expressed in this book are solely those of the authors and not those of the American Academy of Actuaries.

June 1976   THOMAS P. BOWLES, JR.
                               President
                               American Academy of Actuaries

Preface

THIS VOLUME is a textbook on the theory, and to a lesser extent the practice, of pension funding. It is not a general text on all phases of pensions. Matters of purpose, design, tax qualification, and many other pension related issues are clearly outside its scope.

Although the importance of the manner and timing of pension funding has long been realized, no comprehensive treatment of this subject seems to have been attempted. This is not to say that it has been ignored. References to much of the previously published material will be indicated throughout the text. Papers on pension funding appear in some quantity in the recognized actuarial literature, particularly the *Transactions* of the Society of Actuaries and the *Proceedings* of the Conference of Actuaries in Public Practice. The Society of Actuaries has published a volume on pension mathematics. Portions of several books published by the Pension Research Council are devoted to pension funding. Even so, the literature on pension funding is somewhat sparse and largely uncoordinated. References to the literature are listed by number in the List of References at the end of the book.

The funding of pensions has attracted renewed interest and has assumed increased importance with the enactment of the Employee Retirement Income Security Act of 1974 (hereinafter referred to as ERISA). Not only does this legislation establish minimum funding requirements that previously did not exist, but it sets up a class of "enrolled actuaries" to certify that these requirements are met. ERISA's provisions with respect to the Pension Benefit Guaranty Corporation provide additional security to employees, and modify the traditional view as to the liabilities an employer may be assuming when a pension plan is undertaken.

The audience to whom this work is directed primarily is the new group of "enrolled actuaries." As this book is being written the regulations in support of ERISA have not been completed, and the initial group of enrolled actuaries has only recently been established. It seems obvious, however, that enrolled actuaries will not be particularly homogeneous with respect to previous knowledge and experience. It is hoped that this work will be of value to actuaries with little experience in the pension field; but it is directed at the experienced pension actuary as well. The less knowledgeable reader may find parts of this volume difficult, while experienced pension actuaries may find other parts elementary. In any case, this work is written by actuaries and for actuaries; and it necessarily assumes a basic knowledge of actuarial mathematics and a familiarity with the elements of pension plan design.

Readers expecting a cookbook or how-to approach to pension funding will be disappointed. The subject is much too complicated and too subtle to lend itself to superficial treatment. The purpose of this volume is the communication of basic principles, not the detailed description of techniques or a display of mathematical formulas. The authors' aim was a good balance between theory and practice; but where we had to make a choice, we were more likely to emphasize the former.

Chapters 1 through 3 are aimed primarily at establishing general principles. Although they are particularly directed to the less knowledgeable, they may also be of value to employers and union leaders interested in the orderly funding of pension commitments, and to accountants, life underwriters, lawyers, and regulators active in pension matters. More experienced pension actuaries may wish to skip these early chapters, though they should find something of value in Chapter 3's coverage of nomenclature and terminology (see also below).

Chapter 4 establishes an underlying theory based on three mathematical models. Practitioners may be impatient with the theoretical nature of this chapter, and may decide to pass it by.

Chapters 5 through 13 are the heart of this volume, covering actuarial cost methods, actuarial assumptions, adjustments for actuarial gain or loss, the valuation of pension assets, and the necessary adjustments for inflation. These chapters contain most of the tools of the pension actuary, but nonetheless have a strong theoretical flavor.

Accommodations of the theory to fit the practicalities is left to the last four chapters. Chapter 16 in particular is oriented to the practitioner, since it describes the regulatory environment in which the pension actuary does his work. The reader may find himself rejecting some of the ideas from earlier chapters on the grounds that they seem to be outside the current regulatory environment. The authors recognize that what "should be" and what "can be" are sometimes in conflict; but have decided not to ignore what we consider to be worthwhile concepts simply because they have legal difficulties.

A numerical illustration accompanies the text of Chapters 2, 5 through 9, 10, and 13, making it easier for the reader to see the principles as they unfold. The details of the populations, the benefits, and the actuarial assumptions used in the series of illustrations will be found in the Appendix.

Pension funding has been plagued for years by problems of nomenclature and terminology. The authors have paid considerable attention to these problems, especially in Chapter 3, and have endeavored to define confusing terms whenever these terms are first introduced. A summary of special terms, with references as to where these first appear in the text, is included as a Glossary.

There is as yet no established or generally accepted actuarial practice in the pension funding area. There are several problems for which satisfactory solutions have not been found, and many areas in which no consensus has evolved. The authors of this volume consider themselves informed and experienced in pension actuarial matters, but it is *not* our intention to attempt any formulation of generally accepted practice; nor is it our intention to inflict our personal views on others.

Instead, this book is offered under the basic premise that advances in theory and in explanation will lead to improved practice. The authors hope to concentrate on the objective, rather than the subjective, aspects of pension funding, and to keep value judgments to a minimum. In short, we have attempted to provide a textbook and reference work, in the hope that it will be a positive influence toward better understanding and reduced confusion in what has become an important area.

The authors have had the benefit of constructive criticism of earlier drafts from a number of actuaries active in the pension field, and have incorporated many of the suggestions received; though whatever views are expressed (and there must be some) are necessarily our own. In particular, this work does not necessarily represent the views of the Society of Actuaries, the American Academy of Actuaries, or the Conference of Actuaries in Public Practice—all of whom are vitally interested in this important subject area.

June 1976   C. L. Trowbridge
                                                  C. E. Farr

Contents

xiii

16. The Regulatory Environment

The Internal Revenue Code and IRS Regulations—Prior to 1974: *Maximum Deductible Contribution. Minimum Funding Requirements. General Situation under Pre-1974 IRS Rules.* Generally Accepted Accounting Principles. The Employee Retirement Income Security Act of 1974: *Minimum Funding Requirements. Maximum Funding Provisions. The Enrolled Actuary and His Responsibilities. Guarantees on Plan Termination.*

17. Actuarial Reports

1

The Pension Funding Problem

THIS BOOK concerns itself with what the authors call the "pension funding problem." Each of the three words, common enough in their usual sense, will have somewhat specialized meanings for the purposes of this volume.

The word "pension" is here limited to benefits provided by *defined-benefit pension* plans. Plans where the benefits to be paid are directly dependent upon the dollars contributed by or on behalf of an individual do not give rise to the problem to which this volume is addressed. Accordingly, this work does not concern itself with money-purchase pension plans, most kinds of profit-sharing or thrift plans, or any other financial arrangement of the defined-contribution type. Defined-benefit plans in the private sector are within the meaning of the word "pension" as it is used here, as are defined-benefit pension plans for governmental employees. Social insurance has characteristics sufficiently different that it is *not* treated in this volume.

The word "funding" as it is employed here also has a somewhat specialized meaning. In the broader sense pension funding is concerned with the amounts and timing of contributions by employer and employee to meet the benefits the plan provides. One of the approaches to pension funding calls for contributions at the same time and in the same amount as benefit payments becoming due. This procedure has come to be called the "current disbursement" or the "pay-as-you-go" arrangement (these terms will be used inter-

1

changeably). Under a broad definition the word "funding" might apply to these as well as to other arrangements. Most authors, however, have used the word in a narrower context, and view the current disbursement arrangement as the absence of (or even the opposite of) pension funding. Clearly those with this view have limited their concept of pension funding to those arrangements where contributions toward a pension plan are timed ahead of the benefits. For the purposes of this volume, the authors choose to think of pension funding in this narrower sense, and will not use the word "funding" in connection with the current disbursement approach. Whenever the broader concept is intended, the word "financing" may be employed instead.

The nature of the pension funding "problem" will be discussed by means of a somewhat circuitous approach. We will first examine current disbursement or pay-as-you-go, the system which by definition does *not* employ the principle of funding. In this examination we will find two major difficulties, and get some insights as to how a funding arrangement can remove or reduce these disadvantages. This route will hopefully give us clues as to the characteristics of an ideal approach to pension funding, as a guide to the actuary's endeavor in this difficult but important area. Pension funding is therefore viewed as a solution to a problem (or set of problems), rather than as something with intrinsic merit.

CURRENT DISBURSEMENT FINANCING

The principles of current disbursement or pay-as-you-go financing are indeed simple. They are illustrated in Figure 1.

Benefits called for by the plan are paid directly by the employer, as a current disbursement out of his operating income, almost as if the retirees were still at work. The benefit payout varies upward as workers retire, and downward as pensioners die, all under the control of the terms of the plan and the actual experience as to retirement and mortality. The Benefit Valve in Figure 1 is representative of this control mechanism.

If the flow through the benefit valve were monitored, the Benefit Graph (Figure 1) would move upward with each new retirement, downward with each death, and would necessarily show some lack of smoothness. It is of importance to note, however, that the benefit

FIGURE 1

Current Disbursement Financing

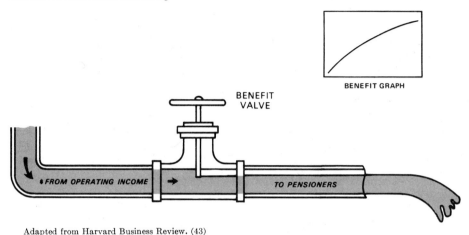

Adapted from Harvard Business Review. (43)

graph is very likely to show an increasing tendency over time, for some or all of the following reasons:

1. In the early years of a plan's existence, the number of pensioners is typically small, but growing. It is not uncommon for a plan to be inaugurated about the time that the oldest employee reaches retirement age. A plan may well have no pensioners initially, but the number of pensioners can be expected to grow with some rapidity as the plan ages.

2. Benefits under defined-benefit pension plans may be initially modest, but later liberalized. Even in the absence of inflationary influences, the pension payroll is likely to grow because of upward changes in the benefits. There is presumably some limit that pensions will never exceed, but many plans today fall far short of their ultimate benefit levels.

3. Even if the number of pensioners and the benefit formula were to become stabilized, inflationary influences are likely to cause the average pension per retiree to grow. If pensions are related to earnings levels, and earnings levels show an increasing trend over time, the growth comes from the replacement effect—i.e., new pensioners have higher pensions than those already pensioned, and particularly higher than the even older pensioners leaving the group by death.

4. A small but growing fraction of today's pension plans have a mechanism for preserving a pensioner's purchasing power. Whether this mechanism is by periodic ad hoc adjustment, or an automatic arrangement geared to a price index, it has the further effect of pushing the benefit graph in an upward direction.

DIFFICULTIES

Pay-as-you-go is clearly the simplest and most straightforward method of pension financing. Were it not for two major disadvantages, current disbursement would presumably be the dominant form. It is well worthwhile to examine these two important difficulties, to see why pay-as-you-go is not more common than it is, and to see why pension funding has developed.

Budgeting of Employer Pension Costs

The tendency under current disbursement financing for employer contributions to increase over time gives rise to the first difficulty. For want of better terminology, the authors have chosen to call this the "budgeting problem."

Under the accrual accounting principle generally employed by business firms, expenses should be reflected on the employer's books when these expenses are incurred. Salaries and wages are charged against the period during which the work was performed, even if the cash payment therefor falls in some different time period. Employer contributions to pensions are very closely related to salaries and wages, representing in the minds of many, a form of deferred compensation. Whether one accepts this rationale or not, it seems that pensions should be charged over the period of employment, not over the period after retirement.

Current disbursement financing charges too little against the earlier years, and hence too much against future years. An expense closely related to today's payroll is being deferred to the future. In a profit making enterprise the result is an overstatement of profits in early years, with a consequent drag on profits in later years. In a nonprofit enterprise a pay-as-you-go pension plan pledges future revenues for work performed today. This is particularly serious if the current disbursement arrangement is entered upon with little appreciation of its increasing cost characteristics.

An example of this budgeting problem is the current disbursement system for paying pensions to members of the armed forces. (39)* The pension payments are a rising charge against the budget for national defense. The defense budget includes a charge to be borne by present taxpayers, though the service giving rise to these pensions was presumably for the benefit of earlier taxpayers. The cost of pension benefits arising from military service performed today will be borne by future generations. At the time when military pensions were first established, and the current disbursement approach adopted, there was very little appreciation of the magnitude of these commitments.

Although pay-as-you-go does not normally have good budgeting characteristics, it should be pointed out that this may not be invariably true. If for any reason the benefit flow as a percent of payroll is stable or declining rather than increasing, current disbursement financing may have better budgeting characteristics than most of the alternatives.

Security of Employee Pension Expectations

The second major difficulty with pay-as-you-go is the dependence of the payment of pensions upon the continuation of employer contributions. Should the flow from the employer completely and finally cease, benefits too must cease (unless some outside source can be tapped). From the pensioner's point of view it is highly unsatisfactory that his pension benefit (which he feels he has earned by work he has performed in the past) is dependent upon the continued willingness and ability of his employer to pay the benefits. Employee pension expectations may well be unfulfilled. (32)

This difficulty, like the first, is not necessarily overwhelming. The likelihood that there may be an interruption in the flow may be considered to be so small as to be negligible. As one example, it is sometimes argued that government employees need not be concerned on this score because of government taxing power. As with any employer, however, the question of willingness, as well as that of ability, enters into the probabilities that pension benefits under a current disbursement system may actually be paid.

---

* References are listed at the end of the book.

THE FUNDED PENSION PLAN

The funded pension plan is at least a partial solution to each of the two important difficulties. The principles of funding can be illustrated by modifying Figure 1.

In Figure 2 a second valve has been inserted between the flow from operating income and the outgoing benefit payments. This one, labeled the Employer Contribution Valve, is "upstream" from the Benefit Valve. Between the two valves is a reservoir, to hold any excess of dollars flowing in over those flowing out.

The employer contribution valve governs the inflow from the employer's operating income. It is controlled by the employer acting with the advice of the pension actuary, or by the terms of a labor-management agreement; and the manner in which this valve is operated becomes the very heart of the pension funding matter. Clearly the opening of this valve has the general effect of building up the level in the reservoir, while its closing will have the reverse effect.

But Figure 2 indicates two other inflows, neither of which operates in a current disbursement system.

One of these is labeled Investment Earnings. This flow is proportional to the level in the reservoir (as indicated by the manner in which the float and the valve operate) and to the rate of investment earnings (represented by the pressure gauge in the investment earnings line). If for any reason the value of the pension assets falls, through default in some security or a stock market slump, investment earnings for a time can be negative. In such an event the flow through the investment earnings line is reversed (and the reading on the gauge becomes negative).

Another inflow is found only in contributory plans, those where the employee himself contributes. Employee contributions are determined by the terms of the plan, and by the number of contributing employees. The employee contribution inflow was omitted from Figure 1, because a contributory noncompulsory plan operating on truly pay-as-you-go principles is not sustainable. One of the corollary advantages of funding is that it makes employee contributions possible. For noncontributory plans the Employee Contribution Valve can be considered to be permanently closed.

The outgo through the benefit valve is little different from that in Figure 1. The plan and the actual experience (as to number and

FIGURE 2

Pension Funding

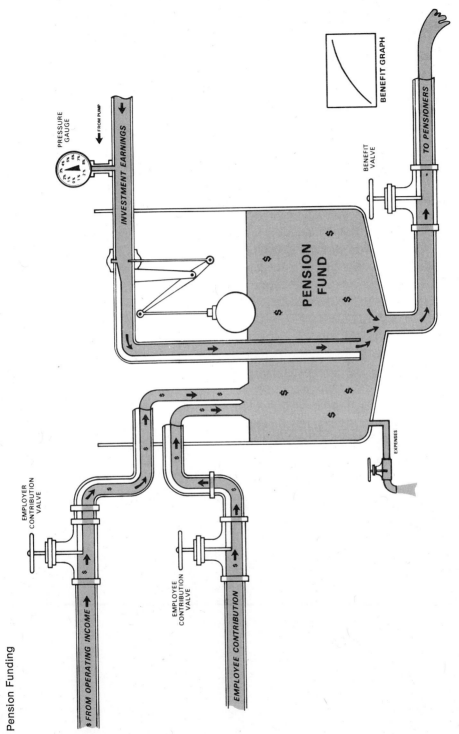

Adapted from Harvard Business Review. (43)

amounts of benefits currently payable) control. The flow through the benefit valve represents, as it did in Figure 1, the dollars payable under a pay-as-you-go arrangement, except that here the flow may be augmented by return of employee contributions on death or withdrawal.

A second potential outgo is a relatively small drain to pay the expenses of keeping the system operating. If such expenses are negligible, or if there is some source of meeting such expenses outside the system, the expense line can be considered to be sealed.

Whether the fund is growing or shrinking at any moment can be ascertained by comparing the sum of the three inflows with that of the two outflows. The level in the reservoir is obviously the accumulated excess, over the time that the system has been in operation, of the total inflow over the total outgo.

HOW FUNDING HELPS

The purpose of modifying the simple current disbursement system shown in Figure 1 into the more complicated funded system represented by Figure 2 is to reduce or eliminate the two basic deficiencies of pay-as-you-go. It will be helpful to note how this can be done.

The charge against the employer has been changed from (1) the flow through the benefit valve (with its typically increasing characteristics), to (2) the flow through the employer contribution valve. To the extent that the contribution valve can be operated to make the employer's contribution fit the principles of good accounting, the first problem has been solved.

At the same time a fund is built up, which fund is committed to the eventual payment of pension benefits. Should the contribution valves be closed, pension benefits can continue until the reservoir goes dry. If the fund is of any magnitude whatsoever, its very presence adds to the security of employee benefit expectations; and if the fund is large enough, the second difficulty with pay-as-you-go completely disappears.

A challenge to the pension actuary lies in the fact that the two objectives of pension funding are not entirely compatible—i.e., the best solutions to the budgeting problem are not necessarily ideal in terms of the security of employee expectations. The employer (and his accountant) must necessarily judge a funding arrangement by the characteristics of the contribution graph, whereas the present and former employees are more interested in the reservoir level. The basic problem of pension funding is to meet these sometimes conflicting objectives with as much fairness to both as may be possible. It is fortunate that the advance funding mechanics provides at least a partial solution to both problems.

OTHER REASONS FOR FUNDING

There are doubtless other reasons for the funding of a pension plan, beyond the solution to the two particular difficulties of current disbursement financing. There are also other ways of expressing the two reasons so far identified, one of which is essentially from the employer's viewpoint, the other from the employees'.

Historically much of the attention has been given to the reasons why an employer might want to fund his pension plan. The budgeting viewpoint has not always been emphasized, at least to quite the extent that this presentation does so. Two British actuaries speak of the "equalisation of burdens," meaning the pension burden on various generations of stockholders. (17) McGill refers to what the authors consider the budgeting reason when he speaks of funding acting as a form of employer discipline. (31)

Other reasons for funding from an employer viewpoint that have often been advanced include federal income tax considerations, and the lowering of eventual employer costs by investment earnings on the pension fund. Neither of these reasons is completely convincing, because current disbursement financing has always had satisfactory federal income tax treatment, and because employer dollars invested outside the pension fund are also productive. At least some employers believe they can earn more on investment within their own businesses, even if they must pay tax on these earnings, than they can on pension fund assets.

Advocates of pension funding also point to the greater flexibility afforded the employer if his plan is funded. Employee contributions can be considered, making possible lower employer contributions for the same benefits; and the employer also has more control as to the amount and timing of his contributions if the plan is funded.

The employee oriented reasons for pension funding have always existed, but they have come to the foreground only rather recently. The thrust of the long legislative development which culminated in the passage of ERISA is all in this direction. The concern for workers whose pension expectations are thwarted by a plan termination after inadequate funding has led to the establishment of the Pension Benefit Guaranty Corporation. A new reason now advanced for pension funding is to avoid an undue drain upon the guaranty fund. (31) An even more convincing reason is that ERISA has, with a few minor exceptions, made the unfunded defined-benefit pension plan in the private sector illegal.

From the point of view of the public as a whole there is still another reason to encourage the funding of pension plans. Private plans, and some state and local governmental plans, have become a very important source of investment capital, and hence finance a significant part of our economic growth. From the economist's viewpoint this may be the single most important reason for pension funding, but from a wider viewpoint the reasons described earlier largely prevail.

JUDGING A FUNDED SYSTEM

It is not difficult to judge an advance funding arrangement from the point of view of employees and their pension expectations. Employees will clearly be satisfied (with the funding, though not necessarily the benefits) if the assets are, and will remain, at or above the present value of all benefits earned to date. Employees may well be satisfied with a lesser level of funding, if the assets will always be at least equal to the present value of *vested* benefits, since funding is not intended to offer additional protection to pensions that can disappear through termination of employment. Finally, employees can perhaps be expected to understand that the asset levels suggested above can hardly be attained quickly—and that the employer would be extremely reluctant to undertake or to liberalize any defined-benefit pension plan recognizing past employee service if the employer were required to fund at these levels immediately. Rather than secure but clearly inadequate pensions, less secure but more adequate benefits may well be in the employees' interests.

From the point of view of the employer and the employer's accountant, the ideal form of advance funding might be one under which employer contributions are relatively level, in absolute dollar terms or more likely as a percentage of payroll. Additional contributions in the early years of the plan, if required to build the fund to fit employee objectives, may be looked upon as a necessary evil. Many employers have shown a more positive attitude, however, accepting the idea that the additional contributions can properly be made, as an adjustment for the "late start" in the funding process with respect to benefits retroactively granted.

The employer may also have an interest in the degree to which he may vary the flow through the contribution valve, cutting the flow and preserving working capital when it seems advantageous to do so, but opening the valve when he can. Manipulation of the contribution valve to fit cash-flow objectives cannot be expected to improve the budgeting characteristics, although good accounting principles can still be followed if adjustments are made through the employer's balance sheet. (26), (27) If this more complicated procedure is followed, the employer's contribution is greater than or less than the charge against the income statement, and the solution to the budgeting problem is partially divorced from the funding arrangements. In most situations, however, the charge against the income statement is identical with the flow through the employer contribution valve; and when this is true the valve must be operated to solve both the budgeting and the employee security problems. Employer contributions and charges against the employer's operating statement are considered to be identical through most of this volume, though the possibility that they may not be is never forgotten.

2

Projecting the
Pay-As-You-Go Stream

THIS CHAPTER is devoted to the problems and techniques of projecting the benefits. This is exactly equivalent to estimating pension costs under current disbursement financing.

The presence of this chapter at such an early stage may be surprising to students of pension funding. Pay-as-you-go is not a method in common use; and the display of the year-by-year estimates of pension benefits is not a necessary step in the calculation of contributions under the common funding methods.

The reason for including this explanation is largely pedagogical. Until it is clear what factors influence the pay-as-you-go stream, and how assumptions as to these factors can be employed to arrive at estimates of the stream itself, little progress can be made with respect to the more general problem—that of changing the timing of employer contributions via the funding mechanism.

In a typical defined-benefit plan without ancillary benefits, the benefit flow will vary over time depending upon at least the following:

1. The probability of each worker's living to retirement age, so that the pension can begin.
2. The probabilities of his or her dying at various ages after retirement date, since the date of death determines when the pension terminates.
3. The probability that the worker will terminate employment

prior to retirement, thereby losing some or all of the pension he or she might otherwise enjoy.

4. The dollar amount of the pension when and if the worker reaches retirement, which may in turn depend upon:
    a. Salary and service record.
    b. Any options for consideration as to when he or she retires, or as to changing the terms under which the retirement income is paid.

All of these factors depend, for any one person, upon the individual's status as of the date of the estimate being made—first as to whether he or she is still employed, has left employment because of retirement, or has left employment prior to retirement with a vested benefit—second as to the worker's age, years of service, and rate of past and current earnings.

Needed, then, to estimate the stream of benefits arising *from employees who have already been hired* is

1. A census of employees to include age (and, to the extent they affect any of the basic probabilities, other factors such as sex, marital status, and so forth), current salary, salary history, and years of service.
2. A census of pensioners, and vested former employees, to include age and amount and form of pension.
3. Assumptions as to the probabilities of death, withdrawal, retirement, and the election of options.
4. Assumptions as to the course of future earnings.

One of the tools of actuarial science is the mathematics needed to combine the census data and the assumptions to estimate the benefit stream. Another is some knowledge of the underlying probabilities, based largely on past experience. Particularly in choosing the actuarial assumptions, the work of a pension actuary may have aspects of an art as well as those of a science. Chapter 10 will have considerably more to say about actuarial assumptions.

With the tools already indicated, the benefit flow arising from those already hired can be estimated. The graph of such stream is likely to have the general shape shown in the area marked AH (already hired) in Figure 3. The increase in early years is due to some or all of the factors mentioned earlier; but sometime in the future, benefits for those hired before the date of the estimate will begin

FIGURE 3

Current Disbursement Financing

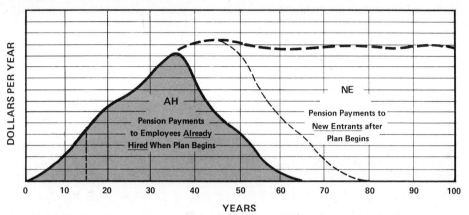

AH area begins at zero, because no employees have reached retirement age at time zero.
NE area shown as zero for 35 years, because all new entrants assumed to be at age 30, and no benefits are to be payable until age 65.

Adapted from Harvard Business Review. (43)

to diminish—reaching zero when (or not long after) the last of this group dies.

To complete the picture, benefits must be estimated for those to be hired sometime in the future. The earliest of these benefits may be quite some years away, but eventually such benefits will replace those in behalf of the initial group.

Estimation of this second portion of the benefit stream is once again dependent upon the basic probabilities. A new uncertainty, however, must be allowed for—the number, the ages, and the initial earnings of those to be employed during each future year. One assumption is that new entrants simply replace the deaths, withdrawals, and retirements from the actively employed group, which is thereby assumed to be constant in size. Such an assumption is not likely to be entirely satisfactory if there is good reason to believe that the employed group will either expand or contract.

The area marked NE (new entrants) in Figure 3 represents benefits payable in behalf of those to be hired after the zero year—i.e., the date of the projection. The AH and NE areas together represent the estimated future benefit flow. As with any projection, the estimate is likely to be more accurate for near-future years than it is for years in the distant future.

Figure 3 gives us a first indication of what may be called the open and closed approaches to pension funding. Its AH and NE areas together present an estimate of pay-as-you-go outlays on an open approach—i.e., future new entrants taken into account. The AH area alone represents the same estimate for a closed group— i.e., future new entrants ignored. The open approach is clearly the more realistic. We shall see later, however, that new entrants can usually be left out of the initial calculation (though hardly ignored) without distortion of the results. When this is true, the open and closed approaches tend to come together.

The closed group terminology, in any case, is something of a misnomer. While it is true that concentration on the AH area alone involves projection of benefits for a closed group, the closing is only temporary. A different group of persons gives rise to a new AH area when the projection is reviewed one period later. The lighter dashed lines on Figure 3 suggest the boundaries of the AH and NE areas when a projection is made 15 years later. The concept of a continually changing closed group is a confusing one; but closed group approaches to pension funding always have this characteristic.

The emphasis in this chapter has been on the estimation of the changing (generally increasing) flow in the benefit stream, and the implied unit has been dollars. For many purposes the benefit stream can be expressed in terms of some other measure—such as annual payroll or number of active employees. The increasing nature of benefits in dollars may have little significance, while increasing benefits as a percentage of payroll may have much more. It may be noted here that the choice of an appropriate unit is always an important aspect of the pension funding problem. We will meet this choice again as funding techniques are discussed.

ILLUSTRATIONS

For the purposes of illustrating the principles of this and later chapters, a hypothetical pension plan has been applied to a hypothetical population of employees and pensioners. The details of both the plan and the population assumed will be found in the Appendix.

Table 1 illustrates the benefit stream arising from the model assumed. (Figure 3 is actually a graphic representation of Table 1.)

TABLE 1

Current Disbursement Financing—Noninflationary Model

	Benefits Paid	
Year	In Thousands of Dollars	As a % of Payroll
1.....................	0	—
2.....................	8	.12
3.....................	22	.32
4.....................	43	.62
5.....................	70	1.00
10.....................	248	3.52
15.....................	457	6.45
20.....................	650	9.15
30.....................	955	13.38
40.....................	1,232	17.39
50.....................	1,239	17.47
Ultimate..............	1,215	17.12

Pension plan and populations as described for noninflationary situation—see Appendix.

TABLE 1A

Current Disbursement Financing—Inflationary Model

	Benefits Paid	
Year	In Thousands of Dollars	As a % of Payroll
1.....................	0	—
2.....................	6	.08
3.....................	19	.25
4.....................	38	.47
5.....................	64	.75
10.....................	279	2.55
15.....................	620	4.42
20.....................	1,054	5.87
30.....................	2,258	7.69
40.....................	4,521	9.52
50.....................	7,224	9.32
Ultimate..............	—	9.17

Pension plan and populations as described for inflationary situation—see Appendix.

It is worthy of note that the model employed for Table 1 simulates a noninflationary economy, under which the benefit stream levels off when the population of both active and retired workers reaches a stationary condition. A model recognizing inflation may be more realistic, and such a model is described in the Appendix, and illustrated by Table 1A. In an inflationary model the benefits, if expressed in dollars, can be expected to rise indefinitely—although they might well level off as a percent of the active payroll.

Note the eventual level is just over 9 percent of payroll in inflationary Table 1A, while it is above 17 percent in the noninflationary Table 1. The direction of this result could be forecast from formula (82) of Bowers, Hickman, and Nesbitt, although the B-H-N model bases the pension on final (rather than final average) earnings and is of an entirely nonvested nature, and hence different from that behind Tables 1 and 1A. (7) Part of the reason why Table 1A benefits as a percentage of payroll are lower than those of Table 1 is the basing of benefits on the final 10-year average pay, which has a stronger depressing effect in the inflationary situation.

3

Principles of Funding

METHODS for establishing and adjusting the employer contribution levels will be the subject of much of the remainder of this volume. Before we turn our attention to specific methods, however, we will do well to recognize certain general principles that pertain to all.

THE EQUIVALENCE OF PRESENT VALUES

An important concept in pension funding is that contributions (and investment earnings) are being substituted for benefits (and expenses). The choice of contribution patterns can be very wide, but the present value of the future contribution stream, together with any fund already built up, must be equal to the present value of the future benefit and expense outflows. Both present values involve a discount for investment earnings or, in other terminology, a recognition of the time value of money. An assumption as to the rate of investment earnings is therefore necessary, an assumption that was not needed in Chapter 2.

Conceptually, the test in the preceding paragraph should be applied in perpetuity—i.e., over all future years. The open-group approach to pension funding applies the test this way. It will be seen that the concept is often modified to require that the present value of the future contribution stream *in behalf of employees already hired*, together with the fund built up, must be equal to the present value of the benefit (and expense) stream in behalf of such employees. The unstated assumption behind this closed-group application is that the present value of the contribution and outgo streams for future new entrants will also be equal. When this un-stated assumption is met, the open and closed-group approaches are in reality the same. The open and closed-group approaches will give different results, however, if for any reason the funding for future new entrants does not meet the equivalence-of-present-values assumption.

The principle of actuarially equivalent present values is also useful in a different context. Whenever an employee is given a choice, but the choices offered are actuarially equivalent, one can be substituted for the other. Although the benefit stream is affected by the choices individuals make, the present value of this stream is not, *provided* that the choices offered are true actuarial equivalents on the actuarial assumptions employed in the present value calcu-lations. The calculation of the present value of benefits is thus easier than the projection of the benefits themselves, because the rates of election of the various actuarially equivalent options can be ignored. This makes the handling of early or late retirement and of the election of joint and survivor forms of retirement income considerably easier. The granting of options that are *not* actuarial equivalents is becoming more common, however, and cannot be so simply handled, involving rates of option election which may be very difficult to assess.

THE ACTUARIAL COST METHOD

A concept very important to the pension funding problem is that of an *actuarial cost method*. The actuarial cost method is the plan under which contributions are to be determined, or (if different) accounting charges are to be accrued. It can also be viewed as the arrangement under which the totality of pension costs is assigned to specific time periods. In the context of Chapter 1 and an earlier portion of this chapter, the actuarial cost method is the plan by which the substitution of contributions (and investment earnings) for benefits (and expenses) is to be effected. These three definitions of an actuarial cost method are intended to be identical in every sense except the words in which they are expressed.

Earlier pension literature used the term *funding method* for the same idea. The more modern term is also more satisfactory, empha-sizing that the costing and the funding of pension plans are some-times divorced. The actuarial cost method terminology was developed in the course of a study of pension nomenclature jointly sponsored by the American Risk and Insurance Association and the Pension Research Council. *Actuarial cost method* apparently first appeared in a recognized publication in 1963; and ever since most of the pension literature, particularly that published by the Pension Research Council, has employed this term. (36) At least one reference to *funding method* can be found in ERISA, although the newer term appears there as well. It is unlikely that any distinction is intended.

There are theoretically as many actuarial cost methods as the ingenuity of man can produce; but more practically the methods in common use number not more than a dozen. The better methods have an understandable rationale, and offer reasonably good solutions to the two phases of the pension funding problem (see Chapter 1).

The early pension literature, particularly the 1945 Treasury Bulletin on 23(p), described the methods then common, and gave them short descriptive names such as "unit credit," "entry-age normal," "attained-age normal," "aggregate," "frozen initial liability," and "individual funding to normal retirement age." (47)

In 1952 one of the authors attempted a classification of these older methods, dividing them into Roman-numeraled classes depending upon the relative sizes of the pension funds ultimately built up. (41) Most of the better known methods appeared in Classes III or IV of the Trowbridge classification system, though very minimum funding was indicated as Class I or II, and very heavy funding was put in Classes V and VI.

The pension nomenclature study of the early 1960's, with Professor Dan McGill of the Pension Research Council the guiding influence, reclassified and renamed the more common of the actuarial cost methods. (36) The Pension Research Council classification system emphasized the mathematical form of the calculations, putting together actuarial cost methods employing similar mathematical techniques. More specifically, the Pension Research Council system attempts to classify each actuarial cost method according to three dimensions:

1. *Accrued Benefit* Cost Methods emphasize the pension accrued or earned to date; in contrast to *Projected Benefit* Cost Methods

which use the projected benefits at retirement as the basic mathematical ingredient.

2. *Individual* Cost Methods are those whose results are the sum of results for each covered individual; in contrast to *Aggregate* Cost Methods which are calculated in such a manner that the total results are not rationally assignable to specific individuals.

3. *With Supplemental Liability* Methods isolate a part of the present value of total benefits, assign it (in a sense) to the past, and fund it separately; in contrast to *Without Supplemental Liability* Methods which do not do so.

Despite the valiant efforts some 15 years ago of Dr. McGill and his Pension Research Council and ARIA associates, the problems of nomenclature for actuarial cost methods are still with us. The Pension Research Council classification system has not been fully accepted throughout the pension world, as is evidenced by the absence of most of this terminology in the 1974 pension legislation. ERISA describes six actuarial cost methods (essentially the same six in the 1945 Treasury Bulletin on 23[p]) without using any of the PRC three-dimensional classification system, though the terms "accrued benefit" and "aggregate" are used to label two of the six methods described.

More recently the Pension Committee of the Society of Actuaries has been working to solve the problems of terminology. As this work is being written, the report of this committee is in exposure form only. Only time will tell what the final report will contain, and whether its recommendations will gain acceptance in the pension world.

The authors of this volume are seriously handicapped by the nonresolution of these nomenclature problems. They have no wish to make the situation worse, and they have no easy solutions to offer. In the remainder of this volume the terminology will be as consistent as possible with the terminology used in ERISA, ignoring to a large extent both the Pension Research Council contribution and the recent efforts of the Society of Actuaries Committee on Pensions. As specific terms are introduced, their meaning will be made clear. The glossary appearing toward the end of this volume will also be helpful. When and if the problems of pension funding terminology and nomenclature are resolved, the authors of this work will be pleased to recast *Theory and Practice of Pension Funding* in whatever terms are agreed upon.

The Normal Cost

Any actuarial cost method can be viewed as calling for a normal or regular contribution. The normal contribution arises from the rationale underlying the method, or from the technique employed. In deference to the precedents of earlier pension literature, this book will hereafter use the term "normal cost," even though the authors consider "contribution" as a more satisfactory noun than "cost."

As an example of an actuarial cost method with a clear-cut rationale and a straightforward normal cost, we will here examine what is commonly called the terminal cost method. From other points of view this method is *not* satisfactory, and the method is therefore not commonly employed—but terminal funding is easily described in the simplest of terms, and is therefore useful as an example to introduce the sometimes difficult normal cost concept.

The rationale behind the terminal method is that the funding for each worker shall take place when that worker retires. The normal cost for any time period becomes the present value of the future benefits, summed over all individuals retiring within that time period. No funding in the current period is contemplated for those not yet ready to retire; and funding for those retired before the time period begins is assigned to the past, and hence is not a part of the normal cost for the current period.

Other rationales lead to different normal costs, and hence to other actuarial cost methods. The normal cost might be the sum of the present values of the pension benefits earned by active employees in a particular year (the accrued benefit cost method), or the sum of the level contributions necessary to fund each individual's projected benefit levelly from entry-age to retirement age (the entry-age cost method). Many other possibilities exist. There is a one-to-one relationship between the actuarial cost method and the rationale underlying its normal cost. A specific actuarial cost method is most easily defined in terms of its normal cost.

McGill's without-supplemental-liability methods are a somewhat confusing exception to the preceding discussion. These methods do not separately fund a "supplemental liability," but instead combine the funding of any such amount along with the payment of what would otherwise be considered the normal cost. Some actuaries view these without-supplemental-liability methods as "without normal cost" as well, on the grounds that the underlying normal cost is not separately identified and the term is therefore inapplicable. Others define the normal cost of these methods as the contribution resulting from the "normal" application of the basic formulas. From the latter viewpoint all actuarial cost methods define a normal cost.

In deference to the views of others involved in the pension funding nomenclature problem, but in conflict with the concept of normal cost developed by one of the authors (41), this work will adopt the viewpoint that all actuarial cost methods are associated with a normal cost, and that for the "without" forms of the various cost methods, the normal cost is simply the contribution produced by the mathematics.

The Accrued Liability

The concept represented by the words "accrued liability" is one of the most important to the understanding of pension funding. Unfortunately, the concept has been ill-defined, and is very commonly misunderstood.

Most of the early literature associates the noun "liability" with this concept, modifying this accounting term with various adjectives. Perhaps the most widely used term has been *accrued liability* (and this is the reason that this term has been here adopted), but in addition the following appear in one reference or another:

Actuarial liability.
Past service liability.
Prior service liability.
Supplemental liability.

The last form is that employed as a classifying term in the ARIA-PRC terminology previously noted.

The concept itself has been confusing even to pension actuaries and technicians. Probably the root of the past difficulty lies in the noun "liability." This word appeared in some of the earliest pension literature and in the Treasury Department Bulletin on 23(p). (45), (8), (47) This early IRS Bulletin, which some of the earliest pension actuaries must have had a hand in writing, was the Bible of the U.S. pension practitioners well into the 1950s.

Whatever the terminology, the *accrued liability* at any time is the then present value of all future benefits, less the present value of normal costs for future time periods. It should make no difference as to whether an open-group or a closed-group approach is employed, as long as the benefits for future new entrants are exactly counterbalanced by future normal costs in their behalf.

The Pension Committee of the Society of Actuaries is likely to recommend the term "supplemental present value." This term is an obvious derivative of the prospective definition in the preceding paragraph, and it was deliberately chosen to avoid the "liability" connotation. There is no liability in the usual accounting sense. Neither the pension fund nor the sponsoring employer has any legal liability of this particular magnitude. Although there may be a valid view that the employer assumes certain obligations, legal or moral, when a defined benefit pension plan is entered upon (and the passage of ERISA has made this view more persuasive), only by accident would the accrued liability be a measure of these obligations.

Actually the accrued liability is more closely related to the asset side of the balance sheet. It can be viewed as a "theoretical" level of assets, a level that would now have been reached had certain conditions prevailed in the past. A precise retrospective definition of the accrued liability at any time is the value of pension assets that would now exist if (1) the normal cost under the actuarial cost method chosen had always been made in strict accordance with the rationale underlying the method, (2) any benefits payable under this rationale had been paid, and (3) all actuarial assumptions had been exactly realized.

In fairness to the early pension actuaries, the use of the word liability was natural, in that pension calculations were commonly displayed in balance sheet form. A pension fund obviously has assets, and a counterbalancing item on the liability side is needed to fit the balance sheet format. Actuarial valuations in balance sheet form are still common today, many practicing actuaries believing that such a presentation aids the process of communication. The authors of this volume have no quarrel with presentations of this kind; but nonetheless consider it a huge step forward if the noun "liability" could magically disappear from pension funding literature.

In further development of the accrued liability concept, it is well to note that, under either the prospective or the retrospective definition, the accrued liability is defined in terms of the normal cost. The normal cost is in turn a function of both the actuarial cost method and the actuarial assumptions. It is particularly important that we recognize that the accrued liability is not uniquely determined even if all actuarial assumptions are specified, since it is importantly a function of the actuarial cost method. Some actuarial cost methods develop much larger accrued liabilities than others, and as a result eventually lead to a much larger accumulation of pension assets.

Earlier the terminal cost method was defined in terms of its normal cost. The accrued liability under this cost method is easily seen to be equal to the present value of future benefits for all participants already retired. Under the prospective definition one comes to this result, since for all participants not yet retired the present value of future benefits equals the present value of future normal costs, leaving the present value of benefits for those already retired as the entirety of the accrued liability. Applying the retrospective definition we arrive at the same result, since assets of this amount would now be in the pension fund had the conditions of the retrospective definition been met.

However, it should be clear that the accrued liability is not affected by the *facts* as to the level of assets in the pension fund. The term "unfunded accrued liability" is used to represent any amount by which the actual assets fall short of the theoretical—i.e., the unfunded accrued liability is equal to the accrued liability less the pension assets.

More often than not there exists an unfunded accrued liability (except where a "without supplemental liability" method has been employed). The unfunded accrued liability is best interpreted as assets that would be there (had the conditions been met), but actually are not. Obviously one reason for an unfunded accrued liability is that the third of the three retrospective definition conditions may not have been met—i.e., experience may have been less favorable than assumed. Even experience losses will not give rise to an unfunded accrued liability, however, if corrective adjustments to past contributions have been made along the way.

The common reason for an unfunded accrued liability is the failure of the first condition. If an actuarial cost method does not become effective until *after* the time that a contribution is called for by the rationale underlying the method, there will be an unfunded accrued liability arising simply from the late start.

This concept can perhaps be made clearer by again using the terminal method as an example. The rationale calls for a contribution for each retirement as retirement occurs. It may be, however, that when the pension plan was first adopted, or when it was liberalized, there were workers already retired but nonetheless entitled to the benefits newly granted. Until such time as the appropriate contribution for those already retired is made, there will be an unfunded accrued liability.

What is often thought of as "paying-off the accrued liability" is in reality making a belated contribution, which under the strict application of the actuarial cost method should have been made earlier. It is almost a truism that any plan which has been started recently, or one which has been recently liberalized, will have an unfunded accrued liability, under almost *any* actuarial cost method of the with-supplemental-liability type.

Without-supplemental-liability methods have somewhat different characteristics. In these methods the rationale calls for normal contributions no earlier than the date the actuarial cost method first becomes effective. Since the normal contributions are zero for time periods prior to the date of the establishment of the funding, the accrued liability as of that date must also be zero. The prospective definition gives the same result, since the present values of future benefits and future normal costs are initially in balance. The without-supplemental-liability terminology is something of a misnomer, however, since these methods produce an accrued liability after the first year. In the absence of experience loss, however, they should never produce an unfunded accrued liability.

Experience Gain or Loss

An actuarial cost method is not completely defined until a means of adjusting for actual experience is incorporated. The actuarial assumptions used for the calculation of contributions will never be realized exactly. As the experience emerges, the differences between what has occurred and what was assumed to occur give rise to either an experience gain or an experience loss. The means of recognition of experience gain or loss is an important feature of an actuarial cost method, and one way by which actuarial cost methods are distinguished. The terms actuarial gain or actuarial loss are here employed to have the same meaning as experience gain or loss, though the actuarial gain or loss terminology has occasionally been used to include the effect of a change in actuarial assumptions. Chapter 11 is a discussion of the techniques of handling actuarial gain or loss.

CONSERVATISM IN PENSION FUNDING

The authors associate the word "conservative" with any feature of a funding arrangement that will advance the timing of contributions. Conservative funding is that which occurs at a faster pace. The more conservative of the actuarial cost methods will build up greater accrued liabilities (and when such accrued liabilities are funded, greater assets) than the less conservative. The more rapid funding of an unfunded accrued liability is another example of more conservative funding.

It will be found that conservative actuarial assumptions have the same effect as a conservative actuarial cost method, in that they too will lead to earlier contributions and larger pension assets. The more common view, that conservative actuarial assumptions are those that tend to overstate contribution estimates, while optimistic or liberal assumptions are those more likely to understate the costs, is entirely consistent with the authors' concept.

The use of the word "conservative" in this specialized sense is similar to the use of the same word by the accounting profession. Last-in-first-out (Lifo) inventory accounting under inflationary conditions is more conservative than first-in-first-out (Fifo), in that the former advances charges against earnings or delays the emergence of profit.

To summarize, conservatism in either the actuarial cost method or the actuarial assumptions advances the timing of contributions and thereby increases the assets in the pension fund. This concept of conservatism will be used frequently throughout this volume. No value judgments are intended, however; the word "conservative" is not here intended to have either favorable or unfavorable connotations.

4

Pension Funding Models

THIS CHAPTER DESCRIBES the pension funding process in terms of mathematical models. Obviously the actual process is so complicated and has so much potential variation that it cannot be accurately described by any simple set of mathematical relationships. Models simple enough that the mind can grasp their essentials have nonetheless been developed, though much "realism" is necessarily lost in the oversimplification. Students of pension funding will do well to study these models, not because they give much help with respect to the day-to-day work of the pension actuary, but because they offer insight as to what is going on behind the actuarial calculations.

As stated in the Preface, this chapter is the most theoretical of the seventeen making up this work. Those whose interest lies only in the practice of pension funding may wish to ignore this chapter. Very little of it is really needed as a background for later chapters, with the possible exception of Chapter 13 dealing with pension funding under conditions of inflation.

This chapter will first describe a stationary population, a noninflationary economy, and finally an inflationary economy, all as background for some statements about the pension funding process under various conditions. Three models will then be presented— (*a*) a mature pension fund under noninflationary conditions, (*b*) a mature pension fund under inflationary conditions, and (*c*) an immature pension fund.

THE STATIONARY POPULATION

Assume that death, withdrawal, and retirement rates applicable to a group of employees have remained unchanged over a substantial period of time. Assume further that those leaving employment through death, withdrawal, or retirement have been continually replaced by new entrants at the younger ages, so that the size of the active working group has been constant. Assume that the pension plan has existed unchanged for the entire career of its oldest member (or that the plan and all of its liberalizations were made fully retroactive to all present and former employees). Under all of these conditions, the populations of active workers, pensioners, and former workers with vested pension rights have all become stationary. A stationary population is not only unchanging in size, but its distribution by age is also constant.

A NONINFLATIONARY ECONOMY

Imagine a noninflationary economy, with prices, wage levels, and interest rates constant. The earnings of any particular employee may grow with increasing age and experience, and average earnings of workers may increase with age due to this promotional element. However, as older and higher-paid employees leave active employment they are replaced by younger lower-paid new entrants, with the effect that the overall average earnings per worker remains constant if the population is stationary. A stationary population of active workers, in a constant wage-level economy, implies a constant total payroll. Note that this concept of a noninflationary economy reflects no increased productivity (or at least none of the results thereof flowing to labor). The long-term interest rate under noninflationary conditions is represented by the force of interest δ_1.

AN INFLATIONARY ECONOMY

In contrast to the noninflationary model, imagine an inflationary economy, with prices rising at a constant (geometrical) rate β, and average earnings of workers increasing at a constant rate γ. β and γ are nominal annual rates of increase, compounded momently. Both rates have held for the past, and both continue for the future.

γ is intended to reflect the rate of salary or wage increase at each age, seniority, or experience level, but not the promotional increases that an individual may receive as he moves through these levels. γ includes the gain in real wages (measured by the excess of γ over β) that labor may be enjoying due to increasing productivity.

Assume that under these inflationary conditions a pension fund earns at a constant force of interest δ_2, presumably higher than δ_1 (the otherwise similar rate in a noninflationary environment).

MATURE FUND—NONINFLATIONARY MODEL

Once the accrued liability has been funded and a stationary population has evolved in a noninflationary economy, we find that the inflows to the pension fund and the outflows therefrom are in balance. The contributions, investment earnings, benefits, and expenses have all become constant, as has the fund.

Let C = normal contributions (employer and employee)
$\qquad I$ = investment earnings
$\qquad B$ = benefit payments
$\qquad E$ = expenses
Then $C + I = B + E$.
Furthermore, if F = value of fund assets
$\qquad\qquad\qquad \delta_1$ = force of investment earnings
$\qquad\qquad\qquad$ and C, I, B, and E are viewed as payable continuously
$$I = \delta_1 F$$

The relationship $C + \delta_1 F = B + E$ has been called the Equation of Maturity. (41) It is helpful to recognize that this important equation is independent of the actuarial cost method, applying uniformly to all.

The Equation of Maturity can be analyzed in terms of the relationships between I, $B + E$, and C.

I can take any level between the extremes of 0 and $(B + E)$, depending on the degree of conservatism in the funding process. At the one extreme, current disbursement financing, I is zero, in which case $C = B + E$. At the other, $C = 0$, and $I = (B + E)$. Here contributions are zero and investment earnings on a very substantial fund are equal to benefits + expenses.

Between the extremes lie all of the actuarial cost methods commonly employed, as well as the whole range of theoretical methods not often used.

The conservatism in actuarial cost methods can be measured by the ultimate $I/(B + E)$ ratio, which can range from 0 to 1. It represents the portion of the eventual benefit load paid by investment earnings. Its complement, $C/(B + E)$, is paid by contributions.

MATURE FUND—INFLATIONARY MODEL

Under the inflationary conditions assumed, and assuming further that pension benefits for those retiring in any year y are related to the average earnings over some past period, the initial pension of an individual retiring in year $y + t$ will be larger by a factor of $e^{\gamma t}$ than that of the otherwise similar individual who retired in year y.

Since we are dealing with a stationary population of retired lives, a similar situation will be found with respect to older generations—those reaching age z in year $y + t$ will then enjoy pensions larger by a factor of $e^{\gamma t}$ than those of a t year older generation when they were age z. The aggregate benefits paid to all pensioners will also increase at the momently compounded rate γ.

To this point we have made no assumption as to any pension increases that may become effective after retirement, as might be provided to preserve the purchasing power of the pension. If pensions for those already retired have increased and continue to do so at a constant rate β, then it has been shown that the aggregate benefits B continue to rise at the rate γ as before. (7) Benefits for each individual rise at a rate β, whereas benefits in the aggregate rise at a presumably larger rate γ, the difference being explained by the replacement effect. As older pensioners die they are replaced by new retirements with higher relative benefits. In the special case where $\gamma = \beta$, the replacement effect is zero, but benefits in total rise at rate $\gamma = \beta$.

As the aggregate benefits increase at the rate γ, the normal contributions C do the same, no matter which of the actuarial cost methods is employed. Expenses are not particularly important, but can be viewed as roughly proportional to contributions, and hence also rising at rate γ.

Finally, if the investment earnings on the fund F are to hold their relationship to C and $B + E$—i.e., the level of funding is to be such that the passage of time, once the stabilized condition has been reached, is not to affect the ratio that I, $B + E$, and C bear to each other—it is necessary that F also increase at the rate γ.

In a recent paper presented to the Society of Actuaries, Bowers, Hickman, and Nesbitt (7) show that the Equation of Maturity under an inflationary model can be expressed as

$$C_t + \delta_2 F_t = B_t + E_t + \gamma F_t \tag{1}$$

The contributions, plus interest on the fund, provide the benefits plus expenses, and enough more to build the fund at the rate γ. It can thus be seen that C_t, B_t, E_t and F_t are all increasing at rate γ, and their ratios are not affected.

Certain interesting relationships can be deduced from the equation above. First we note that if $\gamma = 0$, the formula reduces to the noninflationary Equation of Maturity. This we would expect, since the inflationary model with $\gamma = 0$ is identical to the noninflationary model.

Of more interest is the relationship when $\gamma = \delta_2$. We would expect the interest rate δ_2 to exceed the salary inflation rate γ, but if for any reason they were to be equal, $C_t = B_t + E_t$. The contribution equals the benefits plus expenses, and the arrangement degenerates into a special form pay-as-you-go. There is a fund, but the entire interest thereon is needed to build the fund at the required rate γ. The funding has accomplished nothing in lowering long range costs.

Finally, if δ_2 should for any reason fall below γ, and this relationship should persist for some length of time, a question would arise as to the desirability of continued funding. The contributions would need to exceed the benefits plus expenses if the fund is to grow at the γ rate. Clearly the funding would be holding these ultimate contributions up rather than keeping them down, and pressures to dissipate the fund might well develop.

This analysis demonstrates that the case for pension funding as a solution to the budgeting problem suffers a partial breakdown if return on pension fund investment falls short of the rate of growth of the payroll per worker. Even under these not-very-likely conditions, however, it may still be in the employer's interest to maintain the funding level if the rate of return on pension assets exceeds the firm's internal rate of return, after taxes; and from the point of view of the security of employee expectations, funding continues to be highly desirable.

For purposes of illustrating the conservatism in an actuarial cost method, the ratio comparable to the $I/(B + E)$ suggested for the noninflationary model is

$$\frac{I'}{B + E} = \frac{F(\delta_2 - \gamma)}{B + E} .$$

The numerator is the interest in excess of that needed to build the fund. This ratio, like its noninflationary counterpart, has a potential range from 0 to 1; and its complement, $C/(B + E)$, is the portion of the benefits ultimately paid by contributions. Only if γ exceeds δ_2 does $I'/(B + E)$ become negative and $C/(B + E)$ exceed unity.

IMMATURE FUND

The picture before a stationary population is attained, or before the accrued liability is funded, is somewhat different. In its early or immature stages a funded pension plan will typically have inflow well in excess of outgo, and the fund will rise rapidly from its zero starting point.

The initial buildup of a pension fund is a result of two simultaneously operating factors. First, the accrued liability (hereinafter called L) grows, even under noninflationary conditions, as the population matures. Second, the unfunded portion of the accrued liability (U) becomes smaller as the initial accrued liability is funded. If L_t, F_t, and U_t represent the accrued liability and its funded and unfunded portions at time t, then

$$dF_t/dt = dL_t/dt - dU_t/dt. \tag{2}$$

Since the derivative of U_t with respect to t is presumably negative, the last term is positive, and both factors work toward increasing F.

It can be shown (7) that

$$dL_t/dt = \delta L_t + (C'_t - B_t - E_t) \tag{3}$$

where C'_t is the normal contribution at time t, for the actuarial cost method whose accrued liability is L_t. $B_t + E_t$ is the sum of benefits and expenses at time t, and δ is the force of interest assumed in the calculation of C' and L.

It can also be demonstrated that

$$dF_t/dt = \delta F_t + (C_t - B_t - E_t) \tag{4}$$

where

$$C_t = C'_t + C''_t$$

As before, C'_t is the normal contribution, but C''_t is here the additional contribution toward the funding of U_t.

Combining Equations (2), (3), and (4) we find that

$$C''_t = \delta U_t - dU_t/dt \tag{5}$$

C''_t can be interpreted as a contribution, in excess of the normal contribution, to first replace the missing investment earnings and second to reduce U_t (once again dU_t/dt is negative).

Equations (2) through (5) can be considered the Equations of Immaturity. Eventually the accrued liability is funded, and C''_t and U_t become zero. When this occurs, F_t and L_t come together. Eventually the population matures, F_t and L_t become constant (noninflationary model) or constantly increasing (inflationary model). The twin forces of the maturing of the population and the funding of the accrued liability eventually operate to convert the four Equations of Immaturity into the one or the other of the Equations of Maturity.

Although the development of these Equations of Immaturity presuppose an actuarial cost method of the with-supplemental-liability type, they can be transformed and simplified to reflect the without-supplemental-liability methods. In these circumstances, U_t and C''_t are zero for all values of t, $F_t = L_t$, and $C'_t = C_t$. One Equation of Immaturity sums it all up for this type of actuarial cost method.

$$dF_t/dt = \delta F_t + (C_t - B_t - E_t)$$

This equation is simply a restatement of (4).

5

Accrued Benefit Cost Methods

THIS CHAPTER INTRODUCES the first of two families of actuarial cost methods in common use. The second, the entry age cost methods, will be the subject of Chapter 6.

The accrued benefit terminology was among the recommendations of the group studying pension nomenclature in the early sixties. (36) At least this part of their terminology seems to have caught on, and the accrued benefit cost method has become the modern name for what has variously been called unit-credit, single-premium, or step-rate funding. One of the authors in a previous paper assigned these methods to what he called Class III funding, in recognition of their lesser degree of conservatism than the Class IV methods to be discussed in the next chapter, but their greater levels of funding than Class I (pay-as-you-go) or Class II (terminal funding). (41)

THE RATIONALE

Cost methods of the accrued benefit type emphasize the funding in a particular year y of that portion of the ultimate pension benefit earned by a worker in year y. Special arrangements must be made for funding "past-service" benefits—those earned before the funding began, or those increased retroactively by a later plan liberalization.

The concept is easily understood if the plan clearly assigns pieces or units of the ultimate pension benefit to service years. Under a $x per month per year of service formula, $x of monthly pension is earned each year. The concept is also clear enough if the benefit earned each year is $p\%$ of the worker's earnings for that year, resulting in a total benefit of $p\%$ per year of service times career-average earnings. Here the unit assigned to each year is level as a percent of pay though it may be rising in absolute amount.

Complications arise when the benefit is not service related, when maximum or minimum pensions are a part of the benefit formula, when pensions are based on some form of final or final average pay, or when the plan is integrated with Social Security. The accrued benefit cost method is nonetheless applicable to any pension benefit formula, provided only that the plan design determines (usually for purposes of defining withdrawal benefits) the amount of pension earned to any specific date. With the new ERISA requirements for vesting, plans that up to now have not defined pension earned (or accrued) to date will likely be amended to do so.

THE TRADITIONAL FORM

A straightforward application of the accrued benefit rationale results in the traditional form. The amount of pension earned in a particular service year is the excess of (1) the pension to which the worker is entitled if he terminates at the end of that year, over (2) that to which he would have been entitled if he had terminated at the beginning of the year (with both pensions treated as if 100 percent vested, even though in fact they may not be). Under a 1.5 percent per year final (or highest) 5-year average formula, for example, a worker after 10 years might be entitled to 15 percent of $1,050 per month. A year earlier the computation might have been 13.5 percent of $1,000 per month. The pension earned during the year would then be $157.50 − $135.00 = $22.50. The $22.50 is made up of 1.5 percent of $1,000, plus 15 percent of $50. Note that the pension accrued is considerably steeper than earnings, having increased by $\frac{1}{6}$ while the average earnings increased by only $\frac{1}{20}$. This tendency for the accrual of benefits to be steeper than the salary scale is a marked characteristic of final average pay plans, and (perhaps to a lesser degree) of plans with formulas integrated with Social Security.

THE NORMAL COST

The normal cost (sometimes called current service cost) for any year is the present value of benefits earned during the year. In this calculation it is appropriate to discount for interest, mortality, and *nonvested* termination. For any individual worker the normal cost can be expected to rise throughout his or her career, partly because the benefit earned in a year has rising tendencies due to pay increases, partly because present values of deferred pensions increase with age (as each of the three discounts has a shorter time over which to operate).

The sum of normal costs for all workers does not necessarily rise, however. Some retire, others die or withdraw; and their young age replacements have lower present values per dollar of pension, and quite likely have lower earnings and therefore accrue (during the period in question) a lower pension. Even so, if the average attained age of the active employee group is rising, normal costs under the accrued benefit cost method have a tendency to rise, even when expressed as a percentage of payroll. Once the population of active lives is fairly mature, the rising cost tendency should disappear; but it may persist for some time thereafter if wage inflation accelerates.

It is worthy of note that the normal cost so calculated provides for benefits for those who will later terminate while vested, as well as for those who will continue in active service to retirement. The service tables by means of which the calculation is made make no discount for withdrawal after vesting, and only give partial weight to withdrawal when partially vested. Exactly the same results are obtained as if both vested and nonvested terminators were recognized in the service table, and the vested benefits for the former specifically calculated. This simplification is another application of the principle of the equivalence of present values referred to in Chapter 3.

THE ACCRUED LIABILITY

The accrued liability (sometimes called the past service liability) is the present value of all benefits earned (accrued) prior to the date of determination. The calculation is done in exactly the same manner as in the determination of normal costs, except that accrued benefits are valued (instead of current service benefits), and except that benefits for those already retired, or for those who have previously terminated while vested, must be included.

The past service appellation is accurate when employed with respect to this cost method, because the accrued liability is calculated as the present value of all benefits assigned by the terms of the plan to service performed in the past. It is unfortunate that the past service terminology has been sometimes employed to represent the accrued liability under the entry-age methods, where the accrued liability is something entirely different, having no direct connection with the present value of past service benefits.

The accrued liability can be expected to rise as long as the value of new benefits earned, and the increase in present value of benefits previously earned, is not completely offset by the present values disappearing through death, nonvested termination, and the actual payment to pensioners. Only if the population becomes stationary does the accrued liability stabilize under noninflationary conditions, and under inflationary conditions it would be expected to increase indefinitely unless the number of participants (active and retired) falls off.

The initial accrued liability is normally funded separately. One common way of doing this is by means of n level annual payments, such that the value of the payments (discounted at interest only) is equal to the initial accrued liability. Aften n years the accrued liability is fully funded and, if all actuarial assumptions have been exactly realized and there has been no liberalization resulting in an increase in accrued benefits, there will be no unfunded accrued liability. The initial accrued liability has been funded by the n level payments, and the subsequent increase in accrued liability has been funded via the normal (or current service) cost.

If, subsequent to the inauguration of the plan, a benefit increase is granted affecting benefits already earned, an additional accrued liability is created, which establishes a second layer to be amortized over a period of years. Except for such occurrences the unfunded accrued liability is expected to decrease, and will in fact do so if actuarial losses do not occur, or if suitable adjustments are made if they do.

MATHEMATICS

The basic mathematics of the accrued benefit cost method is very simple.

Let $^{y}CS_{x}$ = current service benefits earned during year y by participants age x in year y

^yPS_x = past service benefits earned prior to year y with respect to participants age x in year y

$^yFS_x = \sum_{t=0}^{r-x-1} {}^{y+t}CS_{x+t}$ = future benefits to be earned during and after year y by participants age x in year y

$^yB_x = {}^yFS_x + {}^yPS_x$ = total projected benefits for participants age x in year y

r = retirement age

a = youngest age at entry

Then NC_y, the normal cost for year y, is defined to be

$$\sum_{x=a}^{r-1} {}^yCS_x \cdot {}_{r-x|}\bar{a}_x$$

and AL_y, the accrued liability for year y, is defined to be

$$\sum_{x=a}^{r-1} {}^yPS_x \cdot {}_{r-x|}\bar{a}_x + \sum_{x=r}^{\omega} {}^yB_x \cdot \bar{a}_x$$

The annuity functions are here assumed to be payable continuously (though in the practical case they are likely to be payable monthly). The $\bar{a}$ functions prior to age r are defined by a double-decrement service table (with decrements for death and for non-vested withdrawal) and a force of interest δ. Technically a different service table is needed for each age at entry, if vesting depends on years of service, but many actuaries use a single table for an average entry age. The first term of the accrued liability formula should include the value of vested benefits for those who withdraw before retirement but are not yet retired; and the second term should include the value of pensions already in the course of payment, whether or not termination of employment occurred prior to retirement.

To convince oneself that the AL_y, as so defined, meets the prospective definition of the Accrued Liability found in Chapter 3, it is only necessary to show that the value of all projected benefits, less the present value of future normal contributions, is equal to the present value of the past service benefits. This is obvious from general reasoning, since the normal cost under the accrued benefit cost method is calculated to fund future service benefits as they accrue, and the present value of such future normal contributions must be equal to the present value of future service benefits.

It would be easy at this point to come to the conclusion that the present value of future service benefits is

$$\sum_{x=a}^{r-1} {}^{v}FS_x \cdot {}_{r-x|}\bar{a}_x,$$

where (as in the calculation of both the normal cost and the accrued liability) the discount for employee withdrawal recognizes non-vested termination only. Unfortunately things are not that simple, except in the case where vested terminations can be assumed to be zero. A vested termination, while it does not affect the present value of benefits already accrued when the termination takes place, eliminates the present value of benefits yet to be accrued. The true value of future service benefits is therefore smaller than the

$$\sum_{x=a}^{r-1} {}^{v}FS_x \cdot {}_{r-x|}\bar{a}_x$$

indicated above, though larger than

$$\sum_{x=a}^{r-1} {}^{v}FS_x \cdot {}_{r-x|}\bar{a}'_x,$$

where the prime indicates a discount for both vested and nonvested withdrawal.

THE PRO RATA FORM

The form of the accrued benefit cost method so far described is the traditional form, the only form that exactly conforms with the rationale by which accrued benefit cost methods are defined. In particular, note that the benefit considered to be accrued in a particular time period is determined by the provisions of the plan itself, and not by any theory as to what benefits are appropriately funded in a particular year.

There is another form of the accrued benefit cost method which for funding purposes assigns to each year of service a pro rata part of the projected benefit at retirement, where the projection may (or may not) be based on a salary increase assumption. A worker with thirty years of service at retirement, and a projected benefit at retirement of $300 per month, would be treated for funding purposes as if the pension formula were $10 per month per year of service, even if the actual formula were something entirely different. Except where the formula is actually of the $x per year of service type, the pro rata form of the accrued benefit cost method treats accrued benefits for funding purposes as different (nearly always higher) than accrued benefits for purposes of computing benefits on termination of employment.

A problem in communication arises in this pro rata form, from the confusion between two different definitions of accrued benefits. Otherwise the pro rata form has some characteristics that attract actuaries to the method.

1. It is a more conservative method than the traditional form, building up an accrued liability equal to the present value of accrued benefits defined on the pro rata principle. For plans with $x per year of service as the benefit formula, the pro rata and traditional forms are obviously identical; but in most other cases the pro rata form will have a larger accrued liability, and will lead to a greater buildup of funds.

2. Because the normal cost for every active individual is not, in general, so steeply rising under the pro rata form as under the traditional technique, there may be less tendency for the total normal cost to rise, and greater stability of normal cost may therefore have been achieved.

3. Just as the pro rata form is more conservative than the traditional form in that it builds up a higher level of pension assets, so is it more conservative in a slightly different sense. The technique earlier suggested for handling vested benefits (discounting for nonvested withdrawal only) does not give exact results as it does for the traditional method; but instead introduces an extra measure of conservatism. Always excepting the $x per year of service plan (for which the traditional and pro rata forms are alike), the pro rata form will turn up actuarial gains whenever a vested employee terminates, since the benefit funded in his behalf (based on pro rata principles) is generally larger than the vested benefit to which he is actually entitled.

For those familiar with *A Quantitative Analysis of Actuarial Cost Methods for Pension Plans,* the pro rata form here described is what McGill and Winklevoss call the constant amount (CA) form of the Modified Accrued Benefit Cost Method (MABCM). (34) It is also the form to which reference is made in the exposure draft on present values, distributed in April 1975 by the American Academy of Actuaries Committee on Actuarial Principles and Practices in Connection with Pension Plans.

ADJUSTMENT FOR ACTUARIAL GAIN OR LOSS

There are at least three techniques for actuarial gain or loss adjustment under the accrued benefit cost methods. The most natural is perhaps the "immediate" adjustment technique, under which "gains" are subtracted from, or "losses" are added to, the contribution otherwise due. The calculation of such gains or losses is perhaps most easily done by comparing the *actual* unfunded accrued liability at the end of a period with the amount of *expected* unfunded accrued liability—i.e., that which would have existed had all actuarial assumptions been exactly realized. The expected unfunded accrued liability is the unfunded accrued liability at the beginning of the period, reduced by any contribution in excess of the normal cost, and increased by interest at the assumed investment rate.

As long as there remains an unfunded accrued liability, another technique for actuarial gain or loss adjustment is available. Gains or losses can simply be allowed to accumulate, thereby hastening (if gains predominate) or delaying (if losses do) the time when the unfunded accrued liability reaches zero. Once such condition does occur, however, adjustment for gains must be done some other way. A variation is to spread the actuarial gain or loss over the same period and in the same fashion as the unfunded portion of the initial accrued liability is being amortized.

Probably the most satisfactory approach to gain or loss adjustment, one that avoids any sudden change in the contribution rates but nonetheless is effective in keeping the funding in line with actual experience, is an adjustment of the "spread" type. Further discussion of this kind of actuarial gain or loss adjustment will be delayed to a later chapter.

EVALUATION

Any actuarial cost method must be evaluated in terms of the solution it offers to the two basic problems, and in terms of more practical considerations such as convenience and explainability.

From the point of view of the security of pension expectations, the Accrued Benefit Cost method must be deemed highly satisfactory *once the unfunded accrued liability is reduced to zero.* All of the accrued pension benefits for present and former employees are then funded, including benefits earned but not yet vested. In the event of plan termination, there should be more than enough funds to guarantee all vested pensions. There will not (except in the pro rata form) be enough to provide all accrued pensions, however, even though pensions accrued to date have been funded. This seeming paradox is the result of the discount for employee withdrawal prior to attainment of a vested status.

Some authors on pension matters take rather literally a Treasury Regulation that implies full vesting on plan termination, and hence view this characteristic as a serious shortcoming of the accrued benefit cost method. (34) Others view the rights of nonvested employees as no greater after plan termination than before, and the Treasury Regulation as having the limited purpose of preventing a return of contributions to the employer upon plan termination. The provisions of ERISA seem to support this latter view, inasmuch as there is no intention that the Pension Benefit Guaranty Corporation protect the benefits of nonvested employees.

The authors view the accrued benefit cost method as satisfactory from the viewpoint of security of pension expectations, *provided* the funding of the initial accrued liability is not too long delayed.

The method is less satisfactory as a solution to the budgeting problem. It has been seen that the normal contribution has increasing tendencies, particularly for final average pay plans funded under the traditional approach where the pattern of pension accruals is steep. For this reason the method may be considered not conservative enough. Conservative actuarial assumptions, with a spread adjustment for gains, will do much to minimize this potential weakness; as will use of the more conservative pro rata form.

The contribution under the accrued benefit cost method, consisting of the normal or current service cost plus any contribution toward the accrued liability, is first computed in dollar terms. It is probably good practice, however, to express the result in terms of a percentage of covered compensation (for plans with benefits related to pay) or in terms of dollars per active employee (if benefits are independent of pay). Results expressed in these terms are likely to be more stable than the dollar amounts, and the plan sponsor is less likely to be misled if the focus is on percent of pay or dollars per active employee. Under inflationary conditions, in particular, a percentage of pay emphasis avoids a myriad of problems.

The method is excellent from the viewpoint of simplicity of concept and ease of explanation, provided only that the benefit formula lends itself to allocation of the pension benefit to specific service years. When this is not the case, the rationale for any accrued benefit cost method becomes cloudy, and the calculations awkward. The method has the additional good characteristic that it automatically keeps track of the ratio of assets to the present value of benefits accrued to date, and can easily be arranged to compare the assets with the present value of vested benefits. This latter comparison seems to be required to meet certain requirements of the accounting profession, and gives useful information in any case.

The pro rata form of the accrued benefit cost method is considerably more conservative than the traditional form, and may result in decreasing normal costs, expressed as a percentage of pay. It may be considered too conservative by some, and it suffers from a confused rationale for benefit formulae other than $x per month per year of service. If the distinction can be clearly drawn between accrued benefits for employee termination (or plan termination) purposes and accrued benefits for funding purposes, the pro rata method may find some good use.

CONSERVATISM

The degree of conservatism inherent in the traditional form of the accrued benefit cost method, as measured by the ultimate $I/(B + E)$ ratio (see Chapter 4) appears to be in the range of $\frac{1}{2}$ to $\frac{2}{3}$, if the interest rate is 4 percent. At lower rates of interest this ratio is smaller—at higher rates, larger. The lower end of the range is representative of final average plans, or any other benefit formula where the pension accrual is steep. The upper end of the same range might be where $x per year of service plans might fall, or the pro rata form no matter the benefit formula. In any case, the level of conservatism, as this term is defined in Chapter 3, is less than under the entry age cost methods yet to be discussed.

ILLUSTRATION

Table 2 illustrates the normal costs, the accrued liability and the buildup of funds under the hypothetical plan described in the Appendix, and under the noninflationary model. Thirty-year level funding of the initial $4.7 million of accrued liability is illustrated. The rise in the normal cost as time goes on is the most important weakness demonstrated. The funding reaches the level of the present value of vested benefits after 25 years; and after 30 the level of the value of all accrued benefits is reached.

Table 3 illustrates the pro rata form of the accrued benefit cost method. Since the plan illustrated is of the final average type, the pro rata form builds up greater assets than the traditional form

TABLE 2

Accrued Benefit Cost Method—Traditional Form (in thousands of dollars)

Year	Contribution Normal Cost	Total	Payroll	Total Contribution as % of Payroll	Accrued Liability	Pension Fund
1.............	360	622	6,883	9.04%	5,271	647
2.............	376	638	6,920	9.22	5,865	1,328
3.............	389	651	6,950	9.37	6,481	2,035
4.............	400	661	6,974	9.48	7,111	2,759
5.............	408	670	6,994	9.58	7,747	3,494
10.............	433	695	7,052	9.86	10,864	7,165
15.............	443	704	7,081	9.94	13,610	10,583
20.............	452	714	7,104	10.05	15,854	13,646
25.............	468	730	7,132	10.24	17,712	16,500
30.............	476	737	7,138	10.33	19,233	19,233
31.............	473	473	7,132	6.63	19,459	19,459
40.............	450	450	7,086	6.35	20,010	20,010
50.............	453	453	7,094	6.39	19,737	19,737
Ultimate..........	455	455	7,099	6.41	19,760	19,760

Contributions and benefits payable as of the beginning of each year.
Accrued Liability and Pension Fund calculated as of end of year, prior to contribution and benefit payments then due.
Initial Accrued Liability is 4,708.
Total Contribution for first 30 years includes amortization of Initial Accrued Liability of 262 per year.

TABLE 3

Accrued Benefit Cost Method—Pro Rata Form (in thousands of dollars)

Year	Contribution Normal Cost	Total	Payroll	Total Contribution as % of Payroll	Accrued Liability	Pension Fund
1..............	380	700	6,883	10.17%	6,336	728
2..............	356	675	6,920	9.75	6,952	1,451
3..............	366	685	6,950	9.86	7,589	2,199
4..............	374	693	6,974	9.94	8,237	2,963
5..............	380	700	6,994	10.01	8,891	3,737
10..............	396	715	7,052	10.14	12,072	7,597
15..............	400	719	7,081	10.15	14,854	11,204
20..............	404	724	7,104	10.19	17,119	14,469
25..............	414	733	7,132	10.28	18,973	17,539
30..............	419	738	7,138	10.34	20,461	20,504
31..............	417	417	7,132	5.85	20,680	20,723
40..............	403	403	7,086	5.69	21,219	21,261
50..............	405	405	7,094	5.71	20,961	21,004
Ultimate..........	406	406	7,099	5.72	20,983	21,026

Contributions and benefits payable as of the beginning of each year.

Accrued Liability and Pension Fund calculated as of end of year, prior to contribution and benefit payments then due.

Initial Accrued Liability is 5,747.

Total Contribution for first 30 years includes amortization of Initial Accrued Liability of 320 per year.

illustrated by Table 2. Accrued benefits, as defined by the terms of the plan, are funded after 25 years. In this illustration the gains resulting from the overprovision for benefits upon vested withdrawal have been taken immediately, accounting for the decrease in normal cost in the second year. With this exception, it will be noted that contribution rates, as a percent of payroll, are more stable than those in Table 2.

6

Entry-Age Cost Methods

IN THIS CHAPTER we consider the second family of cost methods commonly used by pension actuaries, the entry-age cost methods. In Pension Research Council terminology these methods are individual with-supplemental-liability forms of the projected benefit cost method. These methods rely upon the projected benefits at retirement (the

$$\sum_{x=a}^{\omega} {}^{y}B_{x}$$

of the preceding chapter), and particularly the present value of these projected benefits, as the basic ingredient in the calculation.

The present value of projected benefits in year y, hereinafter referred to as PVB_{y}, is identical to the present value of the current disbursement benefit stream for all workers, pensioners, and vested terminators, whose date of hire lies in the past. This is the early part of the benefit stream shown in Figure 3 as the Already Hired (AH) segment.

THE RATIONALE

The normal cost, in the traditional form of the entry-age method, is the level amount which would exactly fund for any individual his projected benefit at retirement if it were contributed from date of eligibility (or other date of entry) until retirement date. (A natural modification of the traditional form, calculating the normal cost as a level percent of increasing pay, will be introduced later.) The present value of these normal costs is then subtracted from PVB_y to obtain the accrued liability.

There may well exist an unfunded accrued liability, because in fact normal costs were not paid for the period following date of entry but prior to the time the funding first became effective. The funding of the initial accrued liability is done outside the normal cost, usually by level annual payments over n years.

THE NORMAL COST

The traditional normal cost for any individual becoming newly eligible at age e is the present value of all benefits he may be expected to receive (including benefits he may enjoy if he terminated employment before retirement but after meeting the vesting conditions) divided by the present value of a unit payable annually over his working career. The present values are calculated with discounts for investment earnings, mortality, and employee withdrawal, and possibly with increments for assumed pay increases.

Normal costs remain level with respect to any individual, but the slope of the normal cost in total will be affected by the replacement of employees dying, retiring, or withdrawing. Only if the average age at entry remains constant, there is no change in the aggregate of all benefits being funded, and actuarial assumptions are all realized, will the normal cost in total be level.

In order to increase the probability of stable normal costs some actuaries prefer to calculate normal costs from a single age of entry $\bar{e}$, constant for all employees in the initial group, even though actual entry ages were various. $\bar{e}$ is chosen to approximate the average entry age under present hiring practices, rather than the average entry age resulting from practices in the past. No "error" is involved with respect to the initial employee group, since the entry-at-age-$\bar{e}$ assumption has an effect only on the split of the initial PVB into its two parts, both of which are provided for in the funding arrangements. If $\bar{e}$ is well chosen, normal costs in the aggregate may be more nearly level than if exact entry ages of the initial group were employed. This form of the projected benefit cost method might be called the "entry-age $\bar{e}$" cost method, to contrast it with the more usual "entry-age normal" form. It is easier to calculate, and has some good characteristics, but does not exactly follow the entry-age rationale.

THE ACCRUED LIABILITY

The accrued liability, with respect to those still employed, is the familiar level premium reserve with which life actuaries have always been familiar, but calculated from entry-age, not from the age attained when the funding actually started. It is perhaps most readily computed prospectively—i.e., the *PVB* less the present value of future normal costs. Since the *PVB* includes the benefits for those no longer in active service, the accrued liability for retired lives and the vested terminated is automatically held when the prospective formula is applied.

A retrospective view of the same level premium reserve indicates that the accrued liability is in fact equal to the assets that would now exist if normal costs had in fact been paid from the date of each employee's entry into the eligible group (or from age $\bar{e}$ if the single entry-age technique was employed), if benefit payments had been made in accordance with the rationale, and if all actuarial assumptions had been realized.

It is important to recognize that the accrued liability for the method here under consideration is at a substantially higher level than for the accrued benefit cost methods. The reasons for this are discussed in various places in the actuarial literature and will not be dealt with at great length here. They are related to the normal cost being a level dollar amount, rather than the increasing cost required to fund a level (or increasing) accruing benefit. It is essentially this larger accrued liability that makes the projected benefit cost methods more conservative (see Chapter 3 for the sense in which this word is used) than the accrued benefit cost methods.

MATHEMATICS

The basic mathematics of the traditional entry-age form of the projected benefit cost method can be expressed as follows:

Let ^yB_x = total benefits projected for persons age x in year y.

^yNC_x = entry-age normal costs for active participants age x in year y. For participants entering at age e, this normal cost is

$$B_e \cdot \frac{_{r-e|}\bar{a}_e}{\bar{a}_{e\;\overline{r-e}\,|}}$$

Let r = retirement age

        a = youngest age at entry

Then   Normal cost of
year y $= \displaystyle\sum_{x=a}^{r-1} {}^{y}NC_x$

Present value of
Benefits $(PVB_y) = \displaystyle\sum_{x=a}^{r-1} {}^{y}B_x \cdot {}_{r-x|}\bar{a}_x + \sum_{x=r}^{\omega} {}^{y}B_x \cdot \bar{a}_x$

Present Value of
Future Normal
Costs $= \displaystyle\sum_{x=a}^{r-1} {}^{y}NC_x \cdot \bar{a}_{x\;\overline{r-x}\,|}$

Accrued Liability
of year y $= PVB_y -$ Present Value of Future
Normal Costs

The $\bar{a}$ functions prior to age r are defined by a double-decrement service table and an assumed rate of interest.

The PVB, and hence the accrued liability, will include the benefits already in the payment process, and the value of vested benefits for those who have already withdrawn but have not yet retired. The PVB and the normal cost must also include the present value of benefits for those who have not yet withdrawn, but who may in the future withdraw prior to retirement but after having met the vesting conditions. This piece of the PVB and the normal cost is not at all easy to compute exactly, since it depends on the dollars of benefit vested as well as upon the probability of termination in the vested state.

Many actuaries use a simpler technique to handle vested benefits. Their service table includes no discount for withdrawal beyond the age (exact or approximate) where full vesting occurs. There is then no addition to the PVB or the normal cost to include benefits for future vested quits, since the assumption that there are none has the effect of funding such benefit. It can be shown that this technique is conservative, effectively funding for those employees who terminate while vested a larger deferred pension than they will be entitled to. Although the approximation here encountered is not of sufficient accuracy to provide a good answer to the question of the additional cost of the vesting provision, it is usually deemed satisfactory for determining contribution levels under the entry-age cost methods. An exact cost of vesting is the subject of at least four papers in the Transactions of the Society of Actuaries. (30), (35), (44), (46).

THE LEVEL PERCENT OF PAY FORM

The form of the projected benefit cost method so far described contemplates a normal cost level in dollar amount. Where a salary scale has been introduced in projecting the benefit at retirement, it is perhaps more appropriate to express a normal cost level as a percent of increasing pay.

The mathematics of this form is essentially the same as that of the more traditional form already developed. It is only necessary to introduce the salary scale in the calculation of the temporary annuities. $\bar{a}_{e\,\overline{r-e}|}$ and $\bar{a}_{x\,\overline{r-x}|}$ become the present values of increasing temporary annuities, rather than the level temporary annuities that the symbols imply. A small s will hereafter be placed over the age designation when the annuity increasing with the salary scale is intended.

It can easily be demonstrated that this level percent of pay form is less conservative than the traditional form, all other things being equal. It is, generally speaking, more conservative than the traditional form of the accrued benefit cost method. It may or may not be more conservative than the pro rata form.

ADJUSTMENT FOR ACTUARIAL GAIN OR LOSS

The three general approaches to gain and loss adjustment described for accrued benefit cost methods can be applied with little change to the entry-age cost methods.

The immediate adjustment technique, and the absorption of actuarial gain or loss by the unfunded accrued liability, can be employed exactly as under the accrued benefit cost method. The "spread" technique will be discussed in later chapters.

EVALUATION

Once the unfunded accrued liability under the traditional form of the entry-age cost method has reached zero, the funding must be deemed highly satisfactory from the viewpoint of the employees interested in security in their pension expectations. We have seen that the accrued benefit cost method stacks up well on this score; and the higher level of assets called for by the traditional entry-age method is more satisfactory from the employee viewpoint. The level percent of pay form also gives satisfactory results from an employee viewpoint once the initial accrued liability is funded.

As a solution to the budgeting problem, the entry-age cost methods have excellent characteristics. Normal costs can be expected to be stable, in terms of dollars per employee in the traditional form, or as a percent of payroll in the variation, even if the average attained age of the employee group is changing, though changes in average hiring age may have some effect. If benefits are related to employee earnings, the budgeting problem will be better solved by calculating normal costs as a percent of payroll; and by expressing the results in the percent of payroll form. This is particularly important when inflationary conditions exist.

The conservative nature of the funding pattern under projected benefit techniques may, however, raise the question as to whether overfunding may occur by the time that assets equal the accrued liability. Those who are naturally conservative would defend the method on any one of several grounds, including the proposition that no one is hurt by additional conservatism whereas many may be hurt if assets prove to be too small. Those less cautious may prefer a less conservative funding method, again on any one of several grounds, including the argument that early plan beneficiaries might have received higher benefits if the apparent level of costs had not been so high.

From the viewpoint of simplicity of concept and ease of explanation, many will prefer the accrued benefit cost method. This may be particularly true after the 1974 legislation, since ERISA emphasizes vested accrued benefits.

CONSERVATISM

The degree of conservatism inherent in the entry-age cost methods, as measured by the $I/(B + E)$ ratio, appears to be in the range of $2/3$ to $3/4$ when the interest rate is 4 percent. With a steep salary scale assumption, and the normal cost calculated as level in percent of pay, this ratio would be in the lower end of this range. Again the higher the interest rate, the higher the ratio of ultimate interest earnings to ultimate benefits.

ILLUSTRATION

Table 4 illustrates for the traditional entry-age method the normal costs, the accrued liability and the buildup of funds under the hypothetical plan described in the Appendix, and under the non-inflationary model. Thirty-year funding of the initial $7.9 million of accrued liability is illustrated. Comparison of funds built up with accrued liabilities shown in Table 2 indicates the degree to which benefits earned to date may be overfunded..

Table 5 similarly illustrates the level percent of pay form. In the noninflationary model here illustrated, the results obtained under the level dollar amount and the level percent of pay forms of the entry-age method are not greatly different.

TABLE 4

Entry-Age Cost Method—Level Dollar Amount (in thousands of dollars)

| Year | Contribution | | Payroll | Total Contribution as % of Payroll | Accrued Liability | Pension Fund |
	Normal Cost	Total				
1	317	753	6,883	10.94%	8,471	783
2	317	753	6,920	10.88	9,132	1,589
3	317	753	6,950	10.83	9,805	2,412
4	317	753	6,974	10.80	10,482	3,246
5	317	753	6,994	10.77	11,159	4,087
10	317	753	7,052	10.68	14,413	8,260
15	317	753	7,081	10.63	17,241	12,207
20	317	753	7,104	10.60	19,538	15,865
25	317	753	7,132	10.56	21,387	19,369
30	317	753	7,138	10.55	22,819	22,819
31	317	317	7,132	4.44	23,027	23,027
40	317	317	7,086	4.47	23,558	23,558
50	317	317	7,094	4.47	23,318	23,318
Ultimate	317	317	7,099	4.47	23,340	23,340

Contributions and benefits payable as of the beginning of each year.
Accrued Liability and Pension Fund calculated as of end of year, prior to contribution and benefit payments then due.
Initial Accrued Liability is 7,878.
Total Contributions for first 30 years includes amortization of Initial Accrued Liability of 436 per year.

TABLE 5

Entry-Age Cost Method—Level Percent of Payroll (in thousands of dollars)

Year	Contribution Normal Cost	Total	Payroll	Total Contribution as % of Payroll	Accrued Liability	Pension Fund
1.............	323	738	6,883	10.72%	8,105	768
2.............	325	740	6,920	10.69	8,758	1,560
3.............	326	741	6,950	10.66	9,425	2,370
4.............	327	742	6,974	10.64	10,097	3,192
5.............	328	743	6,994	10.62	10,770	4,021
10.............	331	746	7,052	10.58	14,008	8,137
15.............	332	747	7,081	10.55	16,829	12,025
20.............	333	749	7,104	10.54	19,123	15,618
25.............	334	750	7,132	10.52	20,975	19,050
30.............	335	750	7,138	10.51	22,416	22,416
31.............	334	334	7,132	4.68	22,625	22,625
40.............	332	332	7,086	4.69	23,157	23,157
50.............	333	333	7,094	4.69	22,914	22,914
Ultimate...........	333	333	7,099	4.69	22,936	22,936

Contributions and benefits payable as of the beginning of each year.

Accrued Liability and Pension Fund calculated as of end of year, prior to contribution and benefit payments then due.

Initial Accrued Liability is 7,470.

Total Contribution for first 30 years includes amortization of Initial Accrued Liability of 415 per year.

7

Aggregate Cost Methods

THE 1945 TREASURY BULLETIN on 23(p) describes an "aggregate" cost method. (47) Both the method and the name appear without substantial change in ERISA. For the purposes of this work this method will be called the "original" form of the aggregate cost method, in order to distinguish it from later developed variations of what is essentially the aggregate approach. Because of these later developments it is now appropriate to speak of several aggregate cost methods.

In Pension Research Council terminology these methods would be classified as aggregate rather than individual, and without-supplemental-liability as opposed to with-supplemental-liability. In PRC terminology there are also aggregate with-supplemental-liability cost methods, but these are the subject of Chapter 8.

THE ORIGINAL AGGREGATE

The aggregate method described in the Treasury Bulletin on 23(p) is essentially the spreading of any unfunded present value of future benefits as a level percentage of the future payroll. The closed-group technique is contemplated, and hence potential entrants after the date of valuation are ignored.

Again let PVB_y represent the present value in year y of future benefits, for those already hired by year y. Let PVS_y represent the present value of future salaries (or payroll) for the same group. Then if F_y and S_y represent the pension fund and the annual payroll as of the beginning of year y, the normal cost for year y, as a percentage of payroll, is

$$\frac{PVB_y - F_y}{.01PVS_y}$$

and the normal cost expressed in dollars is

$$NC_y = \frac{PVB_y - F_y}{PVS_y/S_y}$$

The denominator of this expression for normal cost is

$$\frac{\sum\limits_{x=a}^{r-1} S_{x,y}\, \bar{a}^s_{x\,\overline{r-x}|}}{\sum\limits_{x=a}^{r-1} S_{x,y}}$$

where $S_{x,y}$ represents the payroll at age x in year y. This denominator is an average temporary annuity to retirement, where the annuities are increasing if increases in salary are assumed. The calculation of the average temporary annuity for year y weights each attained age x by the payroll for year y at age x. This average temporary annuity will hereinafter be indicated by the symbol

$$\overset{p}{\overline{\bar{a}^s_{x\,\overline{r-x}|\,y}}}$$

where the s indicates that the annuities may be increasing, the p indicates that the payroll has been used as the weighting function, and the y indicates that the average temporary annuity is a function of time.

For the initial calculation F_y is usually zero. Hence, the initial contribution is simply the present value of future benefits multiplied by the reciprocal of the average temporary annuity to retirement.

$$NC_1 = \frac{PVB_1}{\overset{p}{\overline{\bar{a}^s_{x\,\overline{r-x}|\,1}}}}$$

As time passes, however, F_y grows, becoming an ever more powerful subtractive influence in the numerator. NC_y has therefore a tendency to decrease, especially as a percentage of payroll. This decreasing contribution pattern is one of the more important characteristics of the common forms of the aggregate cost method.

At first glance it might appear that the aggregate method would produce level contributions, expressed as a percentage of pay. Indeed it would do so if there were no new entrants, and therefore the closed group approach employed in each valuation were justified by the facts. In the usual situation, however, there are new entrants; and after the initial contribution a different group of individuals is involved each year. Application of a closed technique to a continually changing group can have some surprising results. Aggregate cost methods are an example of those that do not produce identical results under closed and open approaches, since the unstated assumption as to new entrants (see pages 18–19) is not met.

Under aggregate cost methods it is immediately apparent that the accrued liability, if one is to be defined for such methods, is exactly equal to the pension fund. This is a direct result of the definition of the normal cost and the application of the prospective definition for the accrued liability. Since the accrued liability and the pension fund must necessarily be equal, aggregate cost methods never have an unfunded accrued liability.

The original form of the aggregate cost method, and the later developed forms as well, have another important characteristic. Adjustment for actuarial gain or loss is automatic, and it takes place in a certain specified way. Each year a percentage of the experience gain or loss for that year affects the contribution, along with a similar percentage of the previously unrecognized gain or loss from previous years. The percentage for year y is 100 times the reciprocal of the average temporary annuity for year y. The gain or loss for any year is never *fully* recognized, though substantial recognition occurs rather quickly if the average temporary annuity is not too large. Gains and losses automatically offset each other, and fluctuations in experience are automatically smoothed out. This adjustment technique is clearly conservative when experience gains predominate, and unconservative if experience losses prevail.

THE ENTRY-AGE AGGREGATE METHOD

It has been shown that the aggregate method already described can, under certain conditions, be viewed as a special case of the entry-age methods described in Chapter 6. (41)

To make this demonstration it is sufficient to go back to this earlier chapter, and to pick up the expression for the present value of future normal costs under the level percent of payroll form.

$$PVNC_y = \sum_{x=a}^{r-1} {}^{y}NC_x \cdot \bar{a}^s_{x\,\overline{r-x}|}$$

$$= \sum_{x=a}^{r-1} {}^{y}NC_x \cdot \frac{\displaystyle\sum_{x=a}^{r-1} {}^{y}NC_x \cdot \bar{a}^s_{x\,\overline{r-x}|}}{\displaystyle\sum_{x=a}^{r-1} {}^{y}NC_x}$$

$$= \text{Normal Cost} \cdot \bar{a}^{s\,\overline{NC}}_{x\,\overline{r-x}|y}$$

where

$$\bar{a}^{s\,\overline{NC}}_{x\,\overline{r-x}|y}$$

represents an average temporary annuity to retirement age. In the calculation of the average, the weights are the entry-age normal costs at each attained age x.

The above demonstrates that the entry-age normal cost can be viewed as a percentage of the present value of future normal costs, where the percentage is the reciprocal of the average temporary annuity. This is to say that one part of the PVB_y, the present value of future normal costs, is funded each year by payment of this percentage. In the typical entry-age calculation the initial accrued liability, the second part of the PVB_y, is funded by level dollar amounts over n years—but it could be funded by a percentage of the unfunded. The entry-age aggregate method does exactly that, funding a percentage of the unfunded accrued liability (as defined by the entry-age method) each year. The percentage is once again 100 times the reciprocal of the average temporary annuity. Because the percentage tends to hold steady, but it is applied to a continually decreasing unfunded, the contributions to the initial entry-age accrued liability are decreasing in nature, and they never completely vanish.

The entry-age aggregate method is therefore a variation on the original aggregate method where the weighting function of the average temporary annuity is a little different, but otherwise the calculations are identical. In this form the aggregate method is clearly a special case of the entry-age methods described in Chapter 6, with both the entry-age initial accrued liability, and any experience gain or loss, funded automatically in a smoothly decreasing manner.

Table 6 is an illustration of the aggregate cost method, as it is applied to the population and the plan described in the Appendix. Under the specific conditions assumed for this illustration the salary weighting and the entry-age normal cost weighting are the same, and the average temporary increasing annuities represented by

$$\frac{P}{\bar{a}^s_{x\;\overline{r-x}|y}}$$

and

$$\frac{NC}{\bar{a}^s_{x\;\overline{r-x}|y}}$$

are identical. These average temporary annuities start at about the 9.5 level, and slowly decrease to about 9.25 as the active population ages.

Table 6 is thus an illustration of the aggregate cost method, in either its original or its entry-age form. That the entry-age form of

TABLE 6

Aggregate Cost Method—Original or Entry-Age Form (in thousands of dollars)

Year	Contribution	Payroll	Contribution as % of Payroll	Pension Fund
1	1,107	6,883	16.08%	1,151
2	1,055	6,920	15.25	2,287
3	1,007	6,950	14.49	3,402
4	961	6,974	13.78	4,493
5	918	6,994	13.13	5,556
10	744	7,052	10.55	10,380
15	620	7,081	8.76	14,312
20	534	7,104	7.52	17,382
25	474	7,132	6.65	19,778
30	431	7,138	6.04	21,600
31	424	7,132	5.95	21,869
40	377	7,086	5.32	22,773
50	354	7,094	4.99	22,732
Ultimate	333	7,099	4.69	22,936

Contributions and benefits payable as of the beginning of each year.
Pension Fund calculated as of end of year, prior to contribution and benefit payments then due.

the aggregate method is really a special case of the entry-age method can be demonstrated by comparing Table 6 with Table 5. The ultimate contribution, and the ultimate pension fund are the same. Only the amortization of the initial entry-age accrued liability is different. Table 5 includes $415M toward this amortization each year for 30 years, while Table 6 contributes $748M for the first year, decreasing to $413M in the tenth, $201M in the 20th, $21M in the 50th; ultimately the contribution toward the initial liability approaches zero.

THE ACCRUED BENEFIT AGGREGATE

Just as the original aggregate method is closely related to the entry-age cost methods, another member of the aggregate family is similarly related to the accrued benefit cost method. By use of the aggregate cost method mathematics, but with a different (and larger) function replacing the average temporary annuity, the accrued benefit cost method can be reproduced. In the process the initial accrued liability is funded by a decreasing pattern of past service contributions, and experience gains or losses are adjusted for in the same fashion as in the other aggregate forms.

Chapter 5 gives the formulas for the normal cost and accrued liability under the traditional form of the accrued benefit cost method. Subtracting the accrued liability from the present value of all benefits, (PVB_y), we can obtain the present value of future service benefits, which is also the present value of future normal costs. The function we seek is the ratio that the present value of future service benefits bears to the normal cost, which in turn is the present value of current service benefits. This ratio, hereinafter called f_y, is the average over all workers of the ratios of future service to current service benefits, where each individual is weighted into the average in proportion to his own individual normal cost.

The magnitude of f_y depends partly on whether the traditional form or the pro rata form of the accrued benefit cost method is being simulated. For the latter the future service to current service ratio for those age x is simply the number of years to retirement, $(r - x)$, and the f_y an average thereof. The f_y appropriate to the pro rata form is typically lower than that for the traditional form of the accrued benefit cost method, but higher than the average temporary annuity employed in the first described forms of the aggregate cost method.

TABLE 7

Aggregate Cost Method—Accrued Benefit Form (in thousands of dollars)

Year	Contribution	Payroll	Contribution as % of Payroll	Pension Fund
1	651	6,883	9.46%	677
2	668	6,920	9.65	1,390
3	680	6,950	9.78	2,130
4	687	6,974	9.85	2,884
5	691	6,994	9.88	3,646
10	683	7,052	9.69	7,366
15	657	7,081	9.28	10,645
20	636	7,104	8.95	13,351
25	628	7,132	8.81	15,621
30	612	7,138	8.57	17,514
31	603	7,132	8.45	17,806
40	539	7,086	7.61	18,825
50	515	7,094	7.26	18,909
Ultimate	455	7,099	6.41	19,760

Contributions and benefits payable as of the beginning of each year.
Pension Fund calculated as of end of year, prior to contribution and benefit payments then due.

It should be here stated that the accrued benefit form of the aggregate cost method is not well known or commonly employed. It has most of the characteristics of the more familiar aggregate methods, but it is less conservative, and therefore results in lower initial costs and a lower level of assets.

Table 7 illustrates the accrued benefit aggregate in the same manner as Table 6 illustrates the more familiar aggregate form. A comparison of Table 7 with Table 2 indicates that the ultimate situation is no different from that under the traditional form of the accrued benefit cost method. Over the years the accrued benefit initial accrued liability has been amortized, rapidly at first, then slower and slower. f_y starts at 16.2 and decreases, as the population ages, to 13.7. Table 7 does not illustrate experience gain or loss, but these would be adjusted for automatically, raising the contributions if losses prevail, decreasing them if gains do.

THE GENERALIZED AGGREGATE

The previous discussion of the aggregate cost methods indicates that all of these methods can be viewed as the funding, in any year y, of a percentage k of the then unfunded present value of future benefits $(PVB_y - F_y)$. k is 100 times the reciprocal of the average temporary annuity (increasing or level) if the intended level of conservatism is that of the entry-age methods; or 100 times the reciprocal of the average future service/current service benefit ratio if the lower conservatism associated with the accrued benefit cost methods is preferred.

A generalized aggregate approach was once proposed by one of the authors under the title *The Unfunded Present Value Family*. (42) A better title might have been A Generalized Aggregate Cost Method. The author investigated the characteristics of aggregate funding as the k varied from a minimum value b $(b > \delta)$ upward. By proper choice of k the actuary can accomplish any degree of conservatism he desires.

EVALUATION

Aggregate cost methods (as defined here) have some very attractive characteristics. Among these are the simplicity of the concept, the smoothness of contributions, the automatic adjustment for actuarial gain or loss, and the relatively easy computations.

They have not, however, been widely used. One reason is that only the original form is well known, and only this form is specifically recognized in the legal structure. Because this best known form has very high initial contributions, and eventually builds assets to a level that many consider unnecessarily high, the with-supplemental-liability cost methods, commonly thought to permit more flexibility in the contribution patterns, have been more popular. It has been shown that less conservative forms of the aggregate cost methods are equally valid, but it will be difficult to demonstrate that these meet the minimum funding requirements of ERISA.

8

Frozen Initial Liability Methods

THIS CHAPTER DESCRIBES some actuarial cost methods that have, in the view of some actuaries, the best features of the accrued benefit or entry-age cost methods on one hand, and the aggregate cost methods on the other. One of these methods has long been called the frozen initial liability method, and this name has been chosen by the authors to represent all methods of the same type.

RATIONALE

Frozen initial liability methods are essentially identical to one or the other of the methods described in Chapters 5 and 6, except that they employ the gain or loss spreading techniques associated with the aggregate methods of Chapter 7. For the first valuation the concepts and the mathematics are identical to those of the accrued benefit or entry-age methods, but once experience begins to emerge adjustments to normal costs are made via the mathematics of the aggregate methods.

More specifically, an initial accrued liability, as defined by one of the accrued benefit or entry-age methods, is determined. It is to be funded separately, theoretically in any of several ways, but usually as a level dollar amount over n years. The remainder of the PVB_y, what we have called in previous chapters the present value of future normal costs, is to be funded using the aggregate approach.

In Pension Research Council terminology these are aggregate

with-supplemental-liability methods. We shall see that there are at least three methods that fit this description, and conceptually there are many more.

FROZEN INITIAL LIABILITY—ENTRY-AGE FORM

The method that was the first to be described under the frozen initial liability label is a variation on the straightforward entry-age approach. A first-year normal cost is computed, then the present value of future normal costs is obtained, and finally the initial accrued liability is found by subtracting the present value of future normal costs from PVB_y, the present value of benefits.

In the second and subsequent years the same formulas are applied, but in a different order. The present value of future normal costs is obtained by subtracting from the present value of benefits the initial accrued liability (increased with interest at the valuation rate) and the pension fund assets arising from past normal costs. Because pension fund assets are not easily separated into those arising from normal cost payments and those built up in the amortization of the initial accrued liability, it is usually easier to subtract all pension assets, but only the unfunded portion of the initial accrued liability, calculated as if no gains or losses had taken place. This "expected" unfunded is the previous unfunded, decreased by any contribution in excess of the normal cost, and increased by interest at the valuation rate. Finally, the new normal cost is obtained from the present value of future normal costs by dividing by the average temporary annuity. The better theory is to divide by

$$\frac{NC}{\ddot{a}^s_{x\,\overline{r-x}|}}$$

but it is often easier to use the close approximation

$$\frac{p}{\ddot{a}^s_{x\,\overline{r-x}|}}$$

obtainable by dividing the present value of future payroll by the current payroll.

It is left for the reader to convince himself that the same normal cost is produced as in a straightforward entry-age application, except that all experience gain or loss since the last valuation has been spread into future normal costs.

Tables 4 and 5, which purport to be illustrations of the entry-age methods, are also illustrations of the entry-age form of frozen initial liability. There are no differences so long as there are no experience gains or losses; and Tables 4 and 5, like all of the others, are based on experience in exact accord with the actuarial assumptions.

FROZEN INITIAL LIABILITY—ACCRUED BENEFIT FORM

Exactly the same frozen initial liability techniques can be applied to the accrued benefit cost method. Once again the first year calculation determines an initial accrued liability, though in this case the lower initial accrued liability associated with the accrued benefit cost method. Once again the present value of future normal costs is obtained by subtracting the pension fund and the expected unfunded from PVB_y. Finally the new normal cost, which includes an adjustment for experience gain or loss, is obtained from the present value of future normal costs by division. In this case the divisor is the function designated in Chapter 7 as f_y. The gain or loss adjustment technique has more smoothing power than under the entry-age form, because the divisor is larger.

For the same reason as indicated earlier for Tables 4 and 5, Tables 2 and 3 are illustrations of the frozen initial liability method —accrued benefit form—for the no gain or loss situation.

THE ATTAINED AGE NORMAL METHOD

A method that has long gone under the "attained age normal" label is another of the frozen initial liability forms. From the initial present value of future benefits is subtracted the initial accrued liability, computed in accordance with the accrued benefit cost method. The difference is divided by the average temporary annuity, a function associated with the entry-age method rather than the accrued benefit method. This substitution of the average temporary annuity for f_y continues into future years—otherwise the formulas are the same as for the accrued benefit form of the frozen initial liability method. The result is a peculiar combination of the accrued benefit and entry-age methods, with the gain or loss adjustment techniques of frozen initial liability. The initial accrued liability is at the accrued benefit level, but the accrued liability slowly builds until it reaches the level of the entry-age accrued liability. Attained age normal is illustrated in Table 8.

TABLE 8

Frozen Initial Liability Method—Attained Age Normal Form (in thousands of dollars)

| Year | Contribution | | | | |
	Normal Cost	Total	Payroll	Contribution as % of Payroll	Pension Fund
1	613	875	6,883	12.71%	910
2	595	856	6,920	12.37	1,829
3	578	839	6,950	12.07	2,752
4	562	823	6,974	11.80	3,673
5	546	808	6,994	11.55	4,588
10	484	745	7,052	10.56	8,967
15	439	701	7,081	9.90	12,871
20	407	669	7,104	9.42	16,271
25	386	648	7,132	9.09	19,320
30	371	632	7,138	8.85	22,114
31	368	368	7,132	5.16	22,345
40	349	349	7,086	4.93	23,014
50	341	341	7,094	4.81	22,846
Ultimate	333	333	7,099	4.69	22,936

Contributions and benefits payable as of the beginning of each year.
Pension Fund calculated as of end of year, prior to contribution and benefit payments then due.
Initial Accrued Liability is 4,708.
Total contribution for first 30 years includes amortization of Initial Accrued Liability of 262 per year.

A GENERALIZED FROZEN INITIAL LIABILITY METHOD

Just as the aggregate methods can be generalized by letting the percentage k vary, the frozen initial liability methods can be generalized by variation in two dimensions. Not only can the k vary, but the part of the initial PVB that is thought of as an initial accrued liability can be varied as well.

This interesting generalization of the frozen initial liability methods is the subject of a 1967 paper by Taylor. (40) The three frozen initial liability methods described earlier are all special cases.

EVALUATION

The frozen initial liability technique, with its several variations, is a favorite among many pension actuaries. They like both its with-supplemental-liability and its aggregate characteristics, the latter because of its particularly satisfactory adjustment for actuarial gain or loss.

Pension actuaries have not been as aware of the accrued benefit form of the frozen initial liability as the characteristics of the method deserve, just as they have been relatively unaware of the accrued benefit form of aggregate funding. Since the former is an adaptation of the latter, this is not surprising. The attained age normal method, with its accrued benefit initial accrued liability, but its ultimate accrued liability at the entry-age level, is one attempt to get a spread of actuarial gain or loss into the accrued benefit cost method. The accrued benefit form of the frozen initial liability technique probably does this better, but it does not have the same degree of recognition.

9

Other Actuarial Cost
Methods

CHAPTERS 5 and 6 have examined in some detail the two general
types of actuarial cost methods most commonly employed. Each
was found to be a family of methods, rather than a single clearly
defined method. Chapters 7 and 8 have looked into the aggregate
and frozen initial liability methods, which can be viewed as variations on the methods of Chapters 5 and 6.

In this chapter another actuarial cost method will be described,
some observations will be made as to the open group approach, and
the implications of the non-amortization of the initial accrued liability will be examined.

INDIVIDUAL LEVEL PREMIUM METHOD

A method of some practical importance, one that does not fit
conveniently into any of Chapters 5–8, is usually described as the
individual level premium method. It appeared in the Treasury
Bulletin on 23(p) as "individual funding to normal retirement age,"
and it has occasionally been referred to as "attained age level." (47)
Note that use of "attained age" in connection with this method leads
to confusion with the "attained age normal" method of Chapter 8.

Essentially this is the entry-age method, except that the rationale
of the method is modified to call for normal costs for each individual from the later of (1) his or her entry-age, and (2) the
age attained when the plan was put into effect (or a liberalization
was effective). No funding is contemplated prior to the effective

68

date of the actuarial cost method, and consequently there is no initial accrued liability.

This method is the individual without-supplemental-liability form of the projected benefit cost method under Pension Research Council terminology. It has a close kinship to the method called in this work the aggregate cost method, especially the entry-age version. The individual level premium form spreads the initial *PVB for each individual* levelly over the *individual's* future working lifetime, whereas the aggregate method spreads the totality of the *PVB* over the average future lifetime of the totality of workers. The individual level premium method characteristically calls for a higher initial contribution than the aggregate method, but it falls off more rapidly. If no benefit liberalizations occur, the accrued liability reaches the level of the entry-age accrued liability when the last of the original participants retires.

Table 9 is the illustration of individual level premium funding, for the same plan and the same assumptions as employed in Tables 1 through 8. Each individual premium has been computed as a level percent of increasing payroll, and the pattern of funding after 35 years is exactly equivalent to that in Table 5.

TABLE 9

Individual Level Funding—Level Percent of Payroll (in thousands of dollars)

Year	Contribution	Payroll	Contribution as % of Payroll	Pension Fund
1	1,409	6,883	20.47%	1,466
2	1,299	6,920	18.77	2,868
3	1,200	6,950	17.27	4,207
4	1,108	6,974	15.89	5,483
5	1,025	6,994	14.66	6,696
10	722	7,052	10.24	11,896
15	541	7,081	7.64	15,820
20	437	7,104	6.15	18,700
25	381	7,132	5.34	20,840
30	348	7,138	4.88	22,396
31	343	7,132	4.81	22,614
40	332	7,086	4.69	23,151
50	333	7,094	4.69	22,904
Ultimate	333	7,099	4.69	22,936

Contributions and benefits payable as of the beginning of each year.
Pension fund calculated as of end of year, prior to contribution and benefit payments then due.

The individual level premium method is most commonly used for plans employing as the funding medium individual level premium policies of the income endowment or retirement annuity type. Neither salary increases nor employee withdrawal can be anticipated under individual policies, so in insurance applications the method calculates the premium as a level dollar amount based on current pay rather than as a level percent of increasing pay. When salary increases do in fact occur the level premium is increased to fund the additional pension, and the premium increase is calculated as of the then attained age. The resulting premium for any individual is therefore likely to have stair-step characteristics, with the premium tending to increase as salaries rise, but at a faster rate than the salary itself. These increasing contribution characteristics arising from salary increases are partially offset by the generally decreasing contribution characteristics of the method itself; and by actuarial gains arising from the no-withdrawal assumption. Table 9, incorporating a salary increase scale, a discount for withdrawal, and a premium level as a percent of increasing pay, is not particularly realistic as to individual policy pension plans—although both employ individual level premium funding.

OPEN GROUP APPROACHES

All of the actuarial cost methods so far described are of the closed-group type—i.e., at any time only present and past employees are considered in the valuation. In Chapter 2 the possibility of considering future new entrants was suggested. Chapter 3 describes the conditions under which the open and closed-group approaches are essentially the same.

An examination of the rationale behind the methods of Chapters 5 and 6 indicates that the contributions in behalf of future new entrants are intended to be exactly sufficient to provide the benefits for new entrants, and hence the open and closed-group approaches are in reality the same. The methods of Chapters 8, and the methods so far introduced into this Chapter 9, have similar characteristics. The aggregate methods of Chapter 7 are different in this respect, since the contribution in behalf of new entrants appears, on the surface at least, to be redundant.

Mr. Donald Fleischer recently described what he calls the Forecast Valuation Method. (16) This is not an actuarial cost method, as this term is defined in Chapter 3, but it is a powerful technique for illustrating potential future outcomes and for setting funding policy.

Benefits are projected along the lines of Chapter 2, including those arising in the NE (new entrant) sector. Payrolls are similarly projected. Then the buildup of funds arising from contribution rates specified as a level percent of payroll can be calculated, and the results compared with a pre-established funding objective. A computer program is needed, one that has about the same capabilities as that designed for the illustrations in this volume. Tables 1 through 9 are all open group illustrations, but all assume an active work force of constant size, an assumption that may well be unrealistic in practical situations.

Further development of open group approaches to pension funding can be expected.

NONFUNDING OF AN INITIAL ACCRUED LIABILITY

The principle that the accrued liability will eventually be completely funded is inherent in the equations of Chapter 4. Only when the assets in the pension fund reach and remain at the accrued liability level do the equations of maturity apply. Until then at least the interest on the missing assets must be added to the normal cost if the unfunded accrued liability is not to increase.

It is nonetheless valid, from a point of view of pension mathematics, to leave some part of the accrued liability unfunded forever. If D of the accrued liability L is left unfunded, the fund F is equal to $L - D$, and the investment earnings are δD less than they would have been had L been completely funded. If the contribution C is then increased by δD, the missing investment earnings come into the fund through the contribution inlet, and the sum of contributions and investment earnings is as large as before. The equations of immaturity then tell us that the total inflow is enough to pay the benefits and to increase the fund level by the amount of any accrued liability increase.

In the past it has been fairly common practice, under either the accrued benefit or the entry-age methods, to leave some or all of the initial accrued liability unfunded. The contribution then becomes the normal cost plus interest on the unfunded accrued liability. Such a contribution appealed to some employers and accountants as best meeting the budgeting problem (since no especially large payments in early years were required).

It was pointed out by Griffin that the entry-age normal cost, plus interest only on the entry-age accrued liability, will often fund over a reasonable time period the present value of benefits accrued to date. (18) When this is the situation, the approach has excellent budgeting characteristics and yet provides a good degree of employee security. These good characteristics depend, however, upon the immaturity of the initial group, and/or upon some conservatism in the actuarial assumptions. These factors may explain, at least in part, the relatively high level of funding found in a Pension Research Council study, despite the fact that few plans have completely funded their accrued liabilities. (19)

There has been increasing realization, however, that the interest-only approach leaves something to be desired from a point of view of employee security. The Equation of Maturity (Chapter 4) demonstrates that, with respect to a population initially mature, the normal-cost plus-interest degenerates into pay-as-you-go. In the more usual initially immature situation any increase in accrued liability from its initial level is funded, though its initial value is not. The 1974 pension legislation, with its emphasis on the security of pension expectations, seems to require the eventual funding of any accrued liability, though the provisions regarding the alternate minimum funding standard raise questions as to whether this is always required.

While the principle of non-amortization of the initial accrued liability may seem somewhat discredited, it nonetheless has potential application in those situations where overfunding may otherwise exist. If for any reason the accrued liability under the actuarial cost method employed builds to a level well beyond that needed for employee security purposes, consideration might be given to discontinuance of the amortization of the initial accrued liability when a reasonable level is reached, and the holding constant of any remaining unfunded accrued liability by payment of interest thereon only.

One example of the appropriate use of this approach is in connection with the entry-age cost method, which carries an accrued liability considerably higher than the present value of benefits accrued to date. When the actual funding reaches the benefits-accrued-to-date level, any further amortization of the larger entry-age accrued liability might be abandoned, without any ill effect on employee security. Making this procedure legally possible seems to be the purpose of the alternate minimum funding standard in ERISA.

Another example might be in connection with the accrued benefit cost method. If the fund has reached the level of the present value of benefits accrued and vested, the funding of the remainder of the accrued liability (essentially the present value of benefits accrued but not yet vested) might be reduced to interest thereon. The assets, in event of plan termination, would still be enough to pay the accrued and vested benefits of all participants.

10

Actuarial Assumptions

INTIMATELY CONNECTED with the pension funding problem is that of actuarial assumptions. The use of actuarial assumptions has been suggested in earlier chapters, but the implications have not so far been fully developed.

IN GENERAL

One can begin by examining what an actuarial assumption is; and perhaps more to the point, what it is not.

Probably most actuaries would *not* view an actuarial assumption as a "prediction." No one has the power to foresee the future, and an actuary by his very training knows how cloudy any crystal ball must be.

Some actuaries, and many laymen, consider an actuarial assumption as a "best estimate"—an expression of the actuary's opinion that the eventual outcome is as likely to fall on one side of the estimate as the other. The best estimate may arise from an extrapolation of past experience (on the particular group of employees or on similar groups), perhaps with a recognition of past trends (if any are discernible), and with or without modification to take into account changes anticipated for the future.

Because the consequences of erring on the side of additional conservatism appear less unsatisfactory than those of being too optimistic, many actuaries consciously or unconsciously select assumptions on the conservative side of their best estimate. Others prefer to use best estimates throughout, getting any needed conservatism from the actuarial cost method. Still others strive to use best estimates in all the assumptions but one, thereby concentrating their conservatism in a single assumption (e.g., the investment earnings rate) whose properties they best understand.

In many situations an actuarial assumption can hardly be more than an educated guess, particularly where data as to past experience is nonexistent, or where there is little reason to think that the future will reproduce the past.

For the purposes of this volume, an actuarial assumption will be viewed only as an estimating device. The product of the pension actuary's endeavors may be something more than a "what if" statement, but it seldom is more than an appraisal or a valuation (the latter term is the common one). The actuarial assumption is one of the tools used in arriving at the actuary's valuation, which is in turn an estimate.

A contractor who estimates the cost of a building with the aid of an assumption as to how much each bag of cement will cost is using exactly the same technique. There is perhaps one difference—the contractor will be able to determine the actual cost of cement when he buys it. By eliminating the uncertainty as to the cost of cement, he can then modify his overall estimate to make it more accurate. Eventually his estimate is fully replaced by the actual facts.

In pension funding, on the other hand, the actual experience emerges very slowly. The valuation is always dependent upon the actuary's view of the future, with respect to which new information does not necessarily produce more accuracy than the old. The estimating techniques should, however, result in the replacement of the assumption by the actual experience for time periods already elapsed, thereby contributing at least this degree of additional dependability.

One of the bars to clear thinking in the pension funding area is the confusion that sometimes exists between (1) the actuarial assumptions and their effect on the valuation, and (2) the actual experience and its effect on the benefits that will actually be paid. Differences in actual experience affect the emerging benefits in much the same way that differences in actuarial assumptions affect the valuation; but differences in assumptions have no effect on the benefits that will actually be paid, and differences in actual experience have little effect on the actuarial valuation until considerable time has passed.

Peculiarly enough, although differences in assumptions have *no* effect on the pay-as-you-go costs that will eventually emerge, they will have an effect on contributions under any of the funding techniques in use today. The reason for this seeming anomaly is important. The general principle is that conservative actuarial assumptions have exactly the same effect as conservative actuarial cost methods—i.e., they cause employer contributions to be made earlier and hence hasten the buildup of assets.

It should be pointed out that the overall conservatism of the actuarial assumptions cannot be determined by examining any one of them. A conservative interest assumption, combined with an optimistic assumption as to nonvested employee termination rates, may be more or less conservative in total than a best estimate assumption on both. Actuarial gain or loss (see pages 26 and 27) is the composite result of all assumptions, and it is poor analysis to focus exclusively on any one.

ACTUARIAL ASSUMPTIONS—IN THE SPECIFIC

It is helpful to better understanding of the various assumptions the pension actuary is called upon to make, and their relative effects, if each of the more important is examined separately. (23) The remainder of this chapter will look into assumptions with respect to mortality, employee withdrawal, investment earnings, salary or wage scales, retirement age, and expenses. Others, usually of lesser importance and not specifically considered here, include rates of disability and recovery therefrom, rates of election of certain options, and remarriage rates.

ASSUMPTION AS TO MORTALITY

The longer that people live, the larger is the proportion of workers reaching retirement age, and the longer is the period of time over which pensions are payable. Therefore, the assumption of low rates of mortality (or high probabilities of survival) is conservative, and the reverse is optimistic. Only if ancillary death benefits outweigh the primary retirement benefit would the effect be otherwise.

Mortality rates have been under intensive study for many years. They are known to vary by age and by sex particularly, though additional variation by occupation, socio-economic class, geographic area, or selective influences may be present as well. Mortality rates, particularly at the higher ages where they are most important to the pension funding problem, have shown relatively little movement over recent time.

There are several age-sex specific mortality tables in use by pension actuaries, and the results of an actuarial valuation are not particularly sensitive to the rather small differences between such tables. The differences between male and female mortality are quite pronounced, however, and use of a "unisex" table without adjustment is quite likely to be over-conservative if male workers predominate, overly optimistic if females do. Female mortality rates are lower than male at almost every age, and are less than half of male rates in the middle of the age range.

As an indication of the sensitivity of the estimates to mortality alone, the present value of a unit of pension at age 65 is about 15 percent higher for females than for males.

In general, the mortality assumption gives the pension actuary no particular difficulty, because variation within the range of reasonable choice does not importantly affect the contribution estimates. Very recently a unisex table suitable for pension work has been devised, and a way of adjusting it for varying sex composition has been suggested. (15)

ASSUMPTION AS TO EMPLOYEE WITHDRAWAL

The actuarial valuation is not particularly sensitive to employee withdrawal rates *after* the employee meets the conditions for full vesting. The assumption that there will be no vested withdrawal—i.e., that all vested employees remain employed to death or retirement—may not be realistic; but contribution estimates based on this assumption are not distorted to any important degree. Vested withdrawal has some effect upon any estimate of plan benefits, but relatively little effect on the discounted value of the benefit stream.

On the other hand, contribution estimates in an actuarial valuation are very sensitive to employee withdrawal rates *before* an employee meets the full vesting requirement. Compared to the most conservative nonvested withdrawal assumption (i.e., there is no such withdrawal), an assumption that only one half of the new entrants will survive long enough to become vested cuts the estimate of eventual benefits for new entrants by 50 percent.

Unfortunately, the actuary will usually have very little on which to base his withdrawal assumption. Presumably *voluntary* employee withdrawal depends *at least* upon age, sex, length of service, marital status, income level, and the whole gamut of employment practices within the particular firm. Modern computing equipment makes it practical to use withdrawal rates varying by age, sex, and length of service if good data can be obtained; but many actuaries use a simplified approach recognizing only age, or age and sex, counting on length of service differences to be closely correlated with age. *Nonvoluntary* employee withdrawal is a function of all the economic forces that may cause plant closings, layoffs, mergers, or geographical relocation. Only in very unusual cases will appropriate data from the past be available; and even in these situations projection of past results into the future is highly questionable. There are some published withdrawal tables, but they are illustrative rather than realistic. (12), (35), (37)

For all of the above cited reasons, the pension actuary must depend on the general level of realism in the entire set of actuarial assumptions, a well designed technique for the adjustment for actuarial gain or loss, and an understanding with his client that he knows he will be proved wrong, if he is to keep his problems as to employee withdrawal manageable.

INVESTMENT EARNINGS ASSUMPTION

The assumption as to the rate of investment earnings has some special characteristics.

First, it is unique in that it impinges upon the estimates of contribution under any of the actuarial cost methods, but has no bearing whatsoever on the estimation of the pension payout. Most of the other assumptions relate to the benefits to be paid—whereas the investment earnings assumption has to do with the estimation of one of the inflows.

Second, the rate of investment earnings realized over a particular time period is dependent upon the basis for valuing invested assets. Only with respect to straight debt instruments bought, held, and eventually disposed of at par is the investment earnings rate the same as the so-called coupon rate. Nearly all investments have a potential for capital gain or loss, both of which must be at some time reflected in the investment earnings rate. Moreover, the emergence of investment earnings, entirely aside from capital gain or loss, is importantly a function of the way in which assets are valued. Investment earnings and asset valuation techniques are closely bound together, and neither can be considered alone. Chapter 12 will examine this tie in more detail.

Third, the rate of investment earnings can be very volatile over any short time span, and over the long future (to which the assumption must be addressed) the rate of investment earnings is far from clear. Presumably it is a function of the kinds of investment to which the pension fund will be directed, of the timing of the net cash flow into the pension fund, of the continually changing monetary policy of the Federal Reserve, of the supply and demand for funds, of the changing expectations as to inflation, and of the skill (or luck) of investment management.

There are at least two elements of certainty. It is clear that a lower assumption as to investment earnings is the more conservative one. It is also obvious that the sensitivity of the results to the rate of investment earnings depends particularly on the degree of funding.

If there are very few dollars in the pension fund, and if such situation is likely to exist indefinitely, it makes little or no difference to the contribution estimates what the rate of investment earnings may be, now or in the future. This particular assumption interacts strongly with the general level of conservatism in the actuarial cost method and in the other assumptions. When the general level of conservatism is high, investment earnings have a powerful effect on all parts of the actuarial valuation—but they have a considerably reduced effect if an actuarial cost method that builds little funds is employed.

A rule of thumb sometimes used by pension actuaries—that each 1 percent increase (or decrease) in the investment earnings rate has a 24 percent effect in the opposite direction on the rate of contribution—has been explored by Professor Warren Adams. (1) He finds that this approximate rule has some value if it is properly understood. As in other areas, rules of thumb may be useful; but they can also create more problems than they solve.

A special problem with the investment earnings assumption arises from its interaction with the forces of inflation. Economic theory suggests that interest rates are highly correlated with rates of increase of both prices and earnings. The actuary must be on his guard as to the consistency between his assumption as to the rate of interest and the rate of increase in salaries or wages—and, in plans with benefits tied to an index of consumer prices, the rate of price inflation.

SALARY/WAGE ASSUMPTION

Even under no-inflation conditions, there is usually justification for the use of a salary or wage scale in the pension funding calculations. (28) Though salaries or wages per worker are not increasing in the aggregate, there may nonetheless be an upward slope to the earnings graph with advancing age, recognizing increasing skills, longer seniority, or other promotional factors. A study of average salary or wage by age (or service), at a specific time, may throw light on this promotional aspect.

Under conditions of general increase in salary/wage levels, an additional factor is operating, not only steepening the scale for those already employed, but raising the earnings at which new entrants start as well. This general increase factor may in turn be viewed in two parts: (1) a gain in real earnings, brought about by increasing productivity, and (2) a price increase factor, offsetting the depreciation of the monetary unit through price inflation. It appears today that this general wage increase component is more powerful than the underlying promotion component.

The assumptions made with respect to the salary and wage progress of various generations of employees (including new entrants) may have a powerful influence on the estimate of benefits paid, particularly where pension benefits for an individual are based on salary or wages measured at or near their highest point. These assumptions will also have an important effect on the estimates of future payrolls. Results of an actuarial valuation expressed in terms of a percentage of payroll will therefore not be as sensitive to the salary/wage assumption as results expressed in dollar terms.

ASSUMPTION AS TO RETIREMENT AGE

Plans that have a single normal retirement age, with benefits at earlier or later retirement (where permitted) computed from the normal retirement age benefit on the principle of actuarial equivalence, present no problem with respect to a retirement age assumption. Use of the normal retirement age creates little distortion under any of the actuarial cost methods that prefund the benefits. Estimates of the pension payout itself (as opposed to its present value) should take into account the probabilities of early or late retirement.

Plans that offer essentially a range of normal retirement ages, without an actuarial equivalent factor operating, (38) will require an assumption as to what proportion retire at the various ages, or an assumption as to an average retirement age. In the normal range of retirement ages, a unit of pension deferred one year is worth approximately 6 percent less than a unit pension to commence immediately. This gives some indication of the sensitivity of the cost estimates to the retirement age assumption.

The assumption of a younger average retirement age is obviously conservative.

ASSUMPTION AS TO EXPENSES

Most plans will incur some expense properly assignable to the investment function. This may show up in the form of trustee's fees, fees for investment advice, or the investment expense portion of the charges made by an insurance carrier. Such expenses will be provided for automatically if the investment earnings assumption is made on an after investment expense basis.

Other expenses, if any, to be borne by the pension fund can be viewed as being associated with the contributions. If these expenses are enough to matter, they can enter the contribution estimates by loading the latter by an appropriate percent. Some actuaries, however, use instead a flat dollar amount as a noninvestment expense estimate, or consider it to be partly a function of the number of participants.

11

Actuarial Gain or Loss

IF THERE is anything certain with respect to actuarial assumptions, it is that none of them will be realized exactly. The actual experience may differ in either direction from that assumed, in varying degree, and with changes over time. The effects of actual experience being different from that assumed are called experience (or actuarial) gain or loss. Any actuarial cost method, in order to have credibility and viability over a long time frame, must have a preplanned mechanism for adjustment (usually to the contributions, but conceptually at least sometimes to benefits) to reflect experience as it actually develops.

As has been suggested earlier, there are perhaps three different approaches to such adjustment, with the last of them susceptible to considerable variation in detail.

THE IMMEDIATE ADJUSTMENT METHOD

It is theoretically possible, though sometimes inconvenient, to calculate the dollar amount of all actuarial gain or loss since the last adjustment. This amount can then be added to (if losses predominate) or subtracted from (if gains do) the current contribution. The result of this adjustment is that the fund is put in the same position as if all actuarial assumptions had been exactly realized, even though in fact they were not.

As a very simple example, if the fund in year t earns 5 percent when only 4 percent was assumed, the contribution for year $t + 1$ can be reduced by $\frac{1}{5}$ of the interest earned in year t. After payment of the contribution the fund is exactly where it would have been had 4 percent been earned in year t and no adjustment made.

The dollar amount of actuarial gain or loss in a particular time period can most easily be computed, for the methods described in Chapters 5 and 6, by comparing at the end of the period the actual unfunded accrued liability with the expected, where the latter is the unfunded accrued liability that would exist had no actuarial gain or loss occurred during the period. The expected is the unfunded accrued liability at the beginning of the period, decreased by any contributions made in excess of the normal cost, and increased by interest at the valuation rate. Interest adjustments for the timing of any payment toward the unfunded accrued liability are appropriate. If for any reason the normal cost is not paid in full, or if it is made later than the date as of which it was assumed to be payable, the shortfall will become a part of the actuarial gain or loss for the period.

The immediate adjustment technique is theoretically appealing because it keeps the funding "on target," and therefore the dates when certain funding goals will be reached (e.g., the amortization of the accrued liability) can be predicted. The contribution adjustments can, however, be large and erratic, perhaps in one direction one year and in the other the next; and the budgeting problem is not very well solved. Imagine the effect of this technique for gain and loss adjustment when a high percentage of assets is invested in common stocks valued at market, and the Dow Jones average goes from 1,000 to 600, or the reverse.

IRS regulations appear to permit immediate adjustment for gains, but (for purposes of determining maximum deductible contributions) require losses to be spread—presumably on the usual theory that the maximum deductible employer contribution should not be too large.

UNFUNDED ACCRUED LIABILITY ADJUSTMENT

A second approach is to make the adjustment through the timing of the accrued liability amortization. No adjustment to contributions is contemplated as long as there remains an unfunded accrued liability. Instead actuarial gains decrease the unfunded accrued liability and hasten the day that it may reach zero; actuarial losses act to increase the unfunded accrued liability and to delay the date when such goal will be reached. Another approach must be substituted after the accrued liability has been completely funded —unless the very reaching of this goal triggers a plan liberalization and the re-establishment of an unfunded accrued liability.

As long as there is an unfunded accrued liability, this method of adjustment may be quite satisfactory, particularly if the actuarial assumptions prove to be conservative and experience gains prevail. Fluctuations in experience, even large ones, tend to cancel each other out, and the only distortion is in the projected time when the accrued liability may be completely funded. The hastening of the accrued liability amortization is very satisfactory from an employee security point of view, and the budgeting characteristics are generally good.

One would think that the federal government might encourage this approach to actuarial *gain* adjustment, particularly in view of the new emphasis on employee security. This approach does not appear to be officially sanctioned, however. The maximum funding rules seem to require downward adjustment in contributions whenever actuarial gains prevail.

This approach is not so satisfactory when actuarial assumptions prove to be over optimistic, and hence actuarial losses (instead of gains) prevail. Ignoring the actuarial loss in the calculation of the contributions could result in delaying forever the funding of the accrued liability. The unfunded accrued liability might rise, even though a payment toward the amortization of the accrued liability had been made. It is clearly not good practice to combine overly optimistic actuarial assumptions with an adjustment technique unconservative when losses occur. Actuarial losses thought to be of a temporary nature, or particularly losses that simply offset past gains, would seem to be of little concern. Once a pattern of losses is apparent, though, one of the other adjustment techniques seems necessary, or the actuarial assumptions should be strengthened.

SPREADING OF ACTUARIAL GAIN OR LOSS

Any technique that recognizes actuarial gain or loss by adjusting future contributions, but does it over a period of time and hence considerably less rapidly than the immediate adjustment technique, can be considered a spread adjustment method. Many variations are possible. The longer the period of time over which the adjustment is accomplished, the more powerful the spread, the smoother the resulting contributions, and the more conservative the funding (if gains predominate) or the less conservative (if losses prevail).

One approach is to adjust for a single year's gain or loss by spreading as an annuity-certain over a period of n years, much as an initial accrued liability is amortized in the with-supplemental-liability versions of the common actuarial cost methods. This appears to be the approach contemplated in ERISA, the 1974 pension legislation, with an n of 15 (20 for multi-employer plans). This technique becomes very cumbersome, however, as time goes on. A given contribution eventually carries 15 different adjustments, one for each of the most recent 15 years, unless some simplifying device is employed. Determining gain or loss only every three years, combining gain or loss from various years, and spreading the result over some average remaining period, seem to be permitted under ERISA.

More satisfying to many would be recognizing each year $1/m$ ($m > 1$) of any not-yet-recognized actuarial gain or loss, where such recognition takes the form of an addition to or a subtraction from the unadjusted contribution. If m is large, this technique has powerful spreading characteristics—if m is small, the smoothing power is weak. In this technique a single gain or loss is never fully recognized (except in the limit as time approaches infinity), and this characteristic may appear to be a weakness of this approach. It should, however, be noted that *any* spreading technique, while it may result in the eventual full recognition of the actuarial gain or loss for a particular year, is never caught up with respect to all gain or loss experienced in the past.

The aggregate and frozen initial liability forms of both the accrued benefit and entry-age cost methods essentially employ the m approach, with m particularly defined to spread actuarial gains and losses in the same manner as the normal contribution spreads the present value of future normal costs. m is the function designated as f_y in one case, the weighted average temporary annuity to retirement in the other. In both cases m is not necessarily constant, but is not likely to vary widely. Since f_y is generally larger than either form of

$$\bar{a}^s_{x\;\overline{r-x}|}$$

this spread is more powerful under the accrued benefit method than the entry-age.

GAIN AND LOSS ANALYSIS

Although gain or loss adjustment techniques typically handle actuarial gain or loss in toto, with no distinction made as to how much of the resulting gain or loss is attributable to each of the several actuarial assumptions, pension actuaries sometimes perform a gain or loss analysis. Papers by Dreher and Anderson are the most comprehensive in this particular phase of the pension funding problem. (13), (3)

Gain or loss analysis determines, for the period under analysis, the split of the aggregate gain or loss into its various components. In theory there is a one-to-one correspondence between these components and the various actuarial assumptions employed. The analysis is rather difficult if it is carried out accurately and includes all components. A well conceived gain and loss analysis, particularly if it does not force all uncalculated components into a residual or "all other" category, also performs a worthwhile purpose as a check on the accuracy of the calculations.

Under 1975 conditions, the most important components of the aggregate gain or loss are likely to be those associated with investment results and inflation. Substantial actuarial loss from under-recognition of sharply increasing wage and salary levels has been a part of the picture, offset to some extent by actuarial gain due to rising interest earnings on fixed-dollar investment. Other important actuarial loss has occurred in plans with postretirement consumer price indexing because of recent increases in the CPI; and in plans with common stocks in their portfolios due to the depressed stock market.

CHANGES IN ACTUARIAL ASSUMPTIONS

If the actuarial gain or loss adjustment technique is well worked out, and well understood by all concerned, changes in actuarial assumptions may be very seldom required. Even though the actual experience may be deviating considerably from the assumptions, if the assumptions in the aggregate prove to have been slightly on the conservative side, and if the resulting gains are being well handled, the original assumptions may be satisfactory for a long time.

On the other hand, there are obviously situations where changes in actuarial assumptions must be considered. An emerging pattern of actuarial loss is clearly one of these, but there are others. The actuary's credibility may be impaired because one or more assumptions appear unrealistic, even though the assumptions as a whole are proving to be close to the mark.

In any case, the timing and the degree of changes in actuarial assumptions is a matter of judgment. If a change in assumptions is decided upon, the actuary has an obligation to his client to show what the effect of the change may be, as well as to discuss the reasons why the change is being made. Any such change is at best confusing. Since it involves the expectations for the future, and is not directly related to what has actually occurred in the past, an assumption change is analogous to anticipating a *future* actuarial gain or loss. For clear understanding it is important that experience gain or loss, and the effect of a change in actuarial assumptions, not be confused with each other.

12

Valuation of Pension Fund Assets

AN IMPORTANT AREA to which pension actuaries have devoted some, but not sufficient, attention is the determination of an appropriate dollar value of the assets making up the pension fund. (20) It is all too easy to accept the value reported by the holder of these assets (usually a trustee or a life insurance company) without close examination of the rationale on which the value was determined.

The manner in which assets are valued is of direct concern to the pension actuary, because it affects his assumptions, his results, and his recommendations. The calculation of the rate earned on pension assets is a direct reflection of the asset valuation techniques, as is that part of actuarial gain or loss arising from investment results. Overvaluation of assets will make the present and the past look good at the expense of the future, while undervaluation will have the opposite effect. A valuation method that avoids both is fair to all time periods, but as a practical matter such a goal is not easy to achieve.

Examination of asset valuation techniques must start with classification of pension assets by type. The easiest to deal with is cash or the equivalent. More difficult is the long-term fixed-income type of investment, represented ordinarily by bonds, notes, debentures, mortgages, and occasionally by real estate under a long-term lease. Equity investment, especially common stock, has characteristics that make appropriate valuation for pension purposes a somewhat baffling problem.

CASH—OR ITS EQUIVALENT

As long as the pension fund has good financial records there is really no asset valuation problem with respect to cash or its close equivalent.

Bank accounts can be held at the balance shown on either the bank or the trustee's records, after reconciliation for any items in transit.

Savings accounts or certificates of deposit can be similarly held, though adjustment may be appropriate for interest earned but not yet credited.

Treasury notes, commercial paper, and other very short-term indebtedness can be valued at cost, at market, or at the amount of outstanding indebtedness, since all of these measures should be nearly identical.

Cash values of individual life insurance policies are normally payable upon demand, and such policies are appropriately valued at their cash surrender values.

LONG-TERM INDEBTEDNESS

Bonds, debentures, mortgages, and similar debt instruments bearing a fixed interest rate and maturities well into the future can be valued in several ways. The asset value under any of these valuation methods can be viewed as the discounted value of future interest and principal repayments called for by the instrument of indebtedness. Differences between the methods lie in the interest rate employed in the present value calculation.

Amortized Value

If the interest rate at which future flows are discounted is the same as the yield calculated when a security was acquired, the value moves slowly and smoothly from the cost of the security when it first became a part of the pension fund to its ultimate maturity value. The rate of interest realized throughout is the yield initially determined, provided only that all interest and principal payments are made when due. In the particular case where the security was purchased at par, the bond or mortgage will be valued at par, plus a correction for interest accrued, throughout the term.

If the security were acquired above or below the amount of the indebtedness, the premium or discount is amortized over the life of the security.

This method has a lot to be said for it if the expectation is that most securities of this type will be held to maturity. The average initial yield on a portfolio of long-term debt investment can be closely determined, and this average yield will change relatively slowly. If the investment earnings assumption is never far from this average initial yield, substantial actuarial gain arising from investment results will be avoided, and substantial actuarial loss can only occur if there is default.

This method loses much of its rationale if the investment program contemplates substantial trading in this type of security, since every trade causes a change in valuation basis. Moreover, the amortized value method would appear to be inconsistent with an investment earnings assumption based on yield in the current investment market, unless this yield is substantially equal to the rate of current earnings on the present portfolio.

Market Value

An obvious alternate to amortized value is the market value. Publicly offered bonds have a market value, which can at any moment be determined within a rather narrow range by consulting a bond dealer or from transactions reported by the exchanges. Privately placed bonds and most mortgages are less marketable, but even here a market value can be approximated by applying the same principles that determine market values for marketable bonds.

Market values can be very volatile. A typical $1,000 bond with 15 years left to run bearing a 6 percent coupon (payable semi-annually) is worth only $827 when interest rates for bonds of similar term and comparable quality are on an 8 percent basis. A 10 percent coupon bond under similar circumstances is worth $1,173. Any substantial rise in long-term interest rates decreases the market value of long-term indebtedness, whereas a decline has the opposite effect. The longer the term, the more effect a change in interest rates will have on the market value.

If bonds are to be traded frequently, market value is probably a better measure than amortized value. As trades occur, market values will replace the amortized value, even if the latter is the measure while the bond is held. Market value has more "reality" for many investors if their chances of holding to maturity are small. If actuarial gain and loss arising from a sharply changing market value can be tolerated, or if fluctuating values are unavoidable due to deliberate policies that play upon these changes, market value may well be the best choice.

If market values are held, the market interest rate (the yield at which similar securities are sold) might be appropriate as a base for the investment earnings assumption with respect to this portion of the pension assets.

Discounting at the Assumed Interest Rate

A method with great theoretical appeal is the valuation of long-term debt securities by discounting the income stream at the investment earnings rate employed elsewhere in the actuarial valuation. This method basically assumes that investments are to be held rather than traded. If so, it is internally consistent to value the flows into the pension fund (from the stream of interest and principal repayments on long-term debt securities) at the same rate as is used for the outflows from the fund. Under this approach actuarial gain or loss may occur when the security is bought, or when it is called, exchanged, or sold.

Variations

There are obviously other possibilities. Three are here specifically mentioned.

1. A valuation at par is probably the simplest of all, and can be considered an easy approximation to the amortized value if it is the practice to buy bonds only when they are initially offered.
2. A valuation at an average interest rate at which new bonds have been sold over the recent past (e.g., three years) has many of the characteristics of market valuation, but with somewhat dampened volatility.
3. A valuation at the average interest rate which the present portfolio has earned over the recent past, where earnings have been computed based on market values, has somewhat similar characteristics.

COMMON STOCK—OR OTHER EQUITY INVESTMENT

Common stock does not mature, its dividend is not fixed, and there is almost no firm basis for valuation other than that at which the stock is traded. Since the stock market fluctuates markedly from year to year, month to month, and even day to day, market valuation of common stocks held within pension funds is heavily dependent on the exact time as of which the asset values are calculated.

To smooth out fluctuations, thereby making the valuation less dependent upon the climate at a particular moment, averaging techniques can be employed. The arithmetic mean of stock prices at a number of equally spaced points in the recent past is one technique. Some weighting of current market values and the price at which the stocks were acquired is another. Still another is to hold common shares at a value which will produce a predetermined yield from the time the stocks were acquired. The assumption here is that the long run investment return on common stocks is more easily determined than an appropriate asset value.

On the other hand, some actuaries feel that common stock should nearly always be valued at current market, leaving to the actuarial gain or loss adjustment techniques the job of smoothing out the inherent fluctuations. Actuaries of this bent see no reason to treat experience gain or loss arising from investment results differently than other forms of the same phenomenon.

The technique of discounting future asset inflow at the investment earnings rate assumed (suggested earlier for fixed income investment) might theoretically have some application, but there are obvious difficulties. Neither earnings nor dividends can be projected with any great degree of accuracy; and there may be some question as to which of earnings or dividends is the better measure. Only dividends are credited to the pension fund if the stocks are held; but earnings in excess of dividends must in the long run have some upward effect on stock values.

Other pension assets with equity characteristics may present even more complication than common stocks. Preferred stock and convertible bonds have both equity and fixed income features, as does real estate subject to long-term lease. Market values reflect the inherent characteristics, and may be the best measure if a firm market value can be established. Otherwise, an approximation to market value, or a value based on capitalization of the income stream, are the best possibilities.

PENSION ASSETS HELD BY INSURANCE COMPANIES UNDER GROUP ARRANGEMENTS

Pension assets held in the general account of the insurance company are largely based upon long-term fixed income securities, and are likely to be reported to the actuary in terms of what is essentially amortized value. Unless conversion of this asset to cash is likely, use of amortized value would seem to be appropriate, coupled with interest earnings at a rate consistent with that reported by the insurance carrier.

Pension assets held in a separate account of the insurance company are generally reported in market value terms, and usually (though not always) are invested in common stocks. The techniques previously indicated for valuing common stocks can apply.

IN GENERAL

Valuation of pension assets can be one of the more difficult aspects of the pension funding problem. There are no cut and dried answers, because this is one of the areas in which little or no consensus has developed. The authors recognize that this Chapter 12 is little more than a listing of the asset valuation methods in use, and that little guidance is offered as to which may be the most appropriate under specified circumstances.

There may be some general principles involving internal consistency that are worthy of emphasis. One of these is the consistency between the approach to asset valuation and the investment earnings assumption. If it is likely that pension 'fund assets will not be traded, valuation of the interest or dividend and principal repayment streams at the same rate as used for other parts of the valuation is clearly the soundest approach.

Another is related to the consistency between the asset valuation and the techniques of actuarial gain or loss adjustment. Some dampening of volatile market values may be called for if the immediate adjustment of experience gain or loss is employed, while it may be considered unnecessary if a powerful spread technique is used for experience gain or loss. Occasionally smoothing techniques are adopted for the asset valuation, and the results are smoothed again by the gain and loss adjustment process. If so, there is a danger that the effect of significant changes in market values will be spread so far into the future that the level of conservatism in the process as a whole can be brought into question.

As a general rule, high asset values are less conservative than low values, although this appears to violate the general rule that conservative techniques are those that build the size of the pension fund. An explanation of this seeming anomaly is left to the reader.

13

Pension Funding under Conditions of Inflation

CHAPTER 4 introduced a mathematical and conceptual model of a mature pension fund operating under inflationary conditions. It was found that if general wage levels have been and continue to increase at a constant rate γ, the benefits B, the expenses E, the contributions C, and the fund F can all be viewed as increasing at this same rate, and $B + E$, C, and F are in equilibrium. The inflationary Equation of Maturity was found to be

$$C_t + \delta_2 F_t = B_t + E_t + \gamma F_t$$

Although this model is of use in conceptualizing the problem, it does not furnish the theory needed to handle adequately the problems inherent in the funding of pensions under inflationary conditions. In recent years rates of both wage and price inflation have been high, but not at all steady. Investment earnings rates have responded to inflationary pressures, but in a complicated way that defies simple analysis. The relationships between γ, β, and δ seem to be ever changing, making the choice of appropriate assumptions and techniques extremely difficult. The problem is perhaps the most important one facing pension actuaries today; and is therefore worthy of this separate chapter. There is the beginning of an adequate literature on this important matter, but much further development is needed. (4), (7), (17), (25)

MODIFICATION OF BENEFITS AFTER RETIREMENT

Rising prices will obviously create pressure for upward adjustments in the pension benefit for persons already retired. The concept that at least the purchasing power of the pension should be preserved is very strongly held; and the automatic adjustment for changes in consumer prices is now a part of Social Security, of many plans for government employees, and to a much lesser extent of pension plans in the private sector. It is occasionally argued that pensions should increase faster than the Consumers Price Index, on the grounds that standard-of-living increases enjoyed by workers should be shared with those now retired; but this is so far a minority view.

For a plan with automatic adjustment in post-retirement benefits based on changes in the CPI, the funding of such increases is most appropriately handled in the same manner as the funding of the initial amount of pension. Another actuarial assumption is required, that of the long range rate of increase in the CPI. The effect of an assumption that the CPI, and hence the pension benefit, will rise by j percent annually is approximately the same as that of reducing the investment earnings rate *after retirement only* by j percent. The additional contributions required can be substantial. The accompanying table gives some idea of the magnitude of the additional cost.

Ratio of $\ddot{a}_{65}^{i-j}$ to $\ddot{a}_{65}^{i}$

j \ i	5%	6%	7%
2%	1.167	1.157	1.147
3%	1.269	1.252	1.237
4%	1.388	1.362	1.339
5%	1.526	1.489	1.456

Based on 1971 Group Annuity Table of Mortality.

For a plan without automatic adjustment in postretirement benefits, the best procedure is not quite so clear. With no formal commitment to preserve purchasing power for retired employees, the employer may still expect to make periodic upward adjustment in pension benefits for those already retired, but keeps within his control the timing and the amount of any such increases. Probably the normal procedure for funding ad hoc increases is the establishment of a new unfunded accrued liability when the increase is granted, and the amortization of this over a period of years. Such a funding pattern is clearly less conservative than the preretirement funding of postretirement benefit increases, which might be the normal practice if such increases were automatic.

Another approach to the funding of ad hoc increases is the accumulation of actuarial gains in anticipation of such increases. This might well be accomplished in the same manner as suggested earlier —i.e., by reducing the assumed rate of after retirement investment earnings. The resulting gain, if not dissipated by an immediate adjustment technique, would go far toward setting up the additional accrued liability when an increase is actually granted.

MODIFICATION OF SALARY INCREASE ASSUMPTIONS

Under inflationary conditions salary/wage levels are also rising, at a rate equal to the rate of increase in CPI plus the rate of any gain in real earnings. Over the past twenty years salary/wage levels have risen at something like 5 percent annually (of which gain in real wages has been something like 2 percent), though the year-by-year increases have been very erratic. At 1975 rates of CPI increase, wage increases must be very steep indeed if wages in real dollar terms are not to fall off significantly.

The salary scale, that under noninflationary conditions reflected only a promotional, experience, or seniority effect, is steeper under inflationary conditions. Particularly where pension benefits are based on final average pay, or some near equivalent, the steepened salary pattern has a strong upward effect on projected benefits, and hence on estimated contribution levels.

Although rapidly increasing wage/salary levels imply a steep salary scale and a strong upward effect on potential benefits, they also mean an increase in the payroll base from which both employer and employee contributions stem. If contributions are viewed as rising as the payroll rises, because the contribution as a percent of payroll rather than its dollar level becomes the employer's focus, a large part of the inflation in pension benefits will be funded by the automatic increase in contributions as a constant percent is applied to a larger payroll base.

The effects of a steeper salary scale on projected benefits and on contributions, while in the same upward direction, are not exactly offsetting. Under both pay-as-you-go and terminal funding, the normal cost, expressed as a percent of payroll, will be almost invariant to constant rates of increment in salary levels, once a mature state has been reached. Under the accrued benefit or entry-age cost methods, wage/salary inflation will not appreciably affect normal costs, expressed as a percent of payroll, if the benefit formula is of the career average type. For final average plans, however, funded by either accrued benefit or entry-age cost methods, normal costs are likely to be a higher percent of payroll under a steep salary scale than under a flatter one; unless a higher investment earnings assumption is justified.

This phenomenon can be illustrated by the following. If the salary increase scale represents promotional effects only, the normal cost (level percent of pay) for a pension of k percent of final pay, for a new entrant age a earning S_a is

$$\frac{kS_r \cdot {}_{r-a|}\bar{a}_a^{\delta_1}}{S_a \cdot \bar{a}_{a\,\overline{r-a|}}^{s}{}^{\delta_1}}$$

Here the functions are calculated at a force of interest δ_1, representative of long-term interest rates in a noninflationary economy; and the s as a superscript in the annuity factor in the denominator indicates an annuity increasing in accordance with the salary scale S. Now change the salary scale assumption such that the scale is steeper by the annual rate γ, but leave the δ_1 unchanged. The expression for the normal cost, as a percent of continually increasing pay, is

$$\frac{kS_r e^{\gamma(r-a)} \cdot {}_{r-a|}\bar{a}_a^{\delta_1}}{S_a \cdot \bar{a}_{a\,\overline{r-a|}}^{s+\gamma}{}^{\delta_1}}$$

where $S + \gamma$ represents the steeper salary scale. The result is higher than under the noninflationary salary scale, because the numerator has been multiplied by $e^{\gamma(r-a)}$, whereas the denominator has been multiplied by some weighted $e^{\gamma t}$, where $t < r - a$.

MODIFICATION OF INVESTMENT EARNINGS ASSUMPTION

Under inflationary conditions economists would expect higher rates of investment earnings, at least with respect to assets invested in fixed income securities, than when prices and wages are stable.

The interest rate should at least reflect long-term inflation expectations of investors. Whether the full rate of price inflation flows through into additional investment earnings may be a matter of argument, but there is little doubt that interest rates and inflation expectations are positively correlated. It is not nearly so clear whether investment earnings on common stocks also increase with inflation—the recent past appearing to indicate otherwise.

IMPLICIT VERSUS EXPLICIT RECOGNITION OF INFLATION

We have found that, for final average pension plans, the entry-age normal costs as a percent of payroll are higher under the inflationary model than under the noninflationary one, provided there is no change in the assumed investment earnings rate. We have also seen that economic theory leads us to expect that δ_2 (the rate of investment earnings under inflationary conditions) will exceed δ_1 by an amount somehow related to the price inflation rate β. How $\delta_2 - \delta_1$ might relate to γ, the wage inflation rate, is a matter of further conjecture. However, it seems clear that at least part of the increase in the contribution percentage rate brought about by inflation can be offset by the expected additional investment earnings.

In the past most actuaries have not made explicit assumptions with respect to rates of inflation, though inflationary conditions have been prevalent for at least a decade. They have counteracted the resulting under-conservatism in the salary increase assumption by over-conservatism in the investment earnings assumption. This approach has been called the "implicit" recognition of inflation. If wage inflation does in fact occur, higher investment earnings thought to be associated with inflationary conditions are relied upon to prevent substantial actuarial loss. A paper by Arnold is in part an analysis of this approach. (4)

More recently attention has been given to the "explicit" approach, involving an assumption as to β, γ, and δ_2. A paper by Allison and Winklevoss investigates how rates of contribution, expressed as a percent of payroll, are changed by inflation rates similarly influencing the salary increase scale and the rates of investment earnings. (2)

An extension of the Allison-Winklevoss analysis shows that the contribution rate, as a percent of payroll, is invariant under different levels of the price inflation rate β, provided that certain rather stringent conditions are met.

Assume an entry-age normal cost rate p_1 has been computed for a rate of price inflation β_1, with a salary increase assumption (beyond any promotional effects) γ_1, and an interest assumption δ_1.

Then for a higher inflation rate $\beta_2 = \beta_1 + \Delta$ $\Delta > 0$, the contribution rate p_2 will be equal to p_1 if all of three conditions exist:

(a) $\gamma_2 = \gamma_1 + \Delta$

(b) $\delta_2 = \delta_1 + \Delta$

and (c) the difference in inflation rates Δ is passed on to retirees (as it would if the plan provides automatic CPI adjustments).

p_2 will be less than p_1 if (a) and (b) hold, but (c) does not. This is one of the main findings of Allison-Winklevoss.

On the other hand, if an increment in β is only partly reflected in increased earnings on investments, or if it is more than reflected in salary increases, p_2 may well be greater than p_1.

These somewhat complicated relationships make actuaries dubious about the implicit approach to inflation recognition; and they also require that the explicit approach be quite sophisticated. The difficulties with the explicit approach are largely the problems of estimating δ and γ, and particularly the difference between them. The rate of contribution, expressed as a percent of payroll, is extremely sensitive to $\delta - \gamma$; the higher this difference the lower the contribution. Unfortunately there is no real assurance that $\delta - \gamma$ will always be positive. If it should fall to zero or below over any substantial period, Chapter 4 indicates that a part of the case for pension funding collapses.

ILLUSTRATIONS

Tables 1A through 9A are replications of Tables 1 through 9 introduced in earlier chapters. These illustrations are different from their noninflationary counterparts only in that they involve a salary-increase assumption, γ, due to inflationary forces, of 5 percent annually; a postretirement automatic benefit-level increase, β, of 3 percent annually; and an investment earnings rate, δ, of 7 percent. In the noninflationary model these same percentages were 0, 0, and 4 percent, respectively. A 3 percent inflation factor has been added to β and δ, but the addition to γ has been 5 percent. Under these circumstances we would expect entry-age normal costs to rise, not only in dollars, but as a percent of payroll. Comparisons of Tables 4A and 5A with Tables 4 and 5 show that this is indeed the case.

Tables 2B through 9B are further replications, identical to Tables 2A through 9A except that the investment earnings rate is 9 percent. A 5 percent inflation factor has now been added to γ and δ, but the addition to postretirement benefits has been held to 3 percent. Here we would expect entry-age normal costs, expressed as a percent of payroll, to be lower than under the noninflationary model. Comparisons of Tables 4B and 5B with Tables 4 and 5 bear out this expectation. In dollar terms the contributions cross after about 10 years, as the higher payroll catches up with the lower percentage.

For the pay-as-you-go situation (Tables 1), the accrued benefit methods (Tables 2 and 3), the aggregate methods (Tables 6 and 7), the attained-age normal (Tables 8), and the individual level premium method (Tables 9) the effects of adopting an inflationary model are not quite so predictable. Much insight can be gained by a careful study of the tables of this chapter, and comparison with their non-inflationary counterparts.

TABLE 2A

Accrued Benefit Cost Method—Traditional Form (in thousands of dollars)

Year	Contribution		Payroll	Total Contribution as % of Payroll	Accrued Liability	Pension Fund
	Normal Cost	Total				
1.............	317	513	6,883	7.45%	3,129	549
2.............	355	551	7,265	7.58	3,721	1,171
3.............	392	589	7,661	7.69	4,381	1,862
4.............	428	625	8,071	7.74	5,105	2,620
5.............	463	660	8,501	7.76	5,890	3,441
10.............	639	836	10,938	7.64	10,641	8,415
15.............	839	1,035	14,018	7.38	16,683	14,770
20.............	1,105	1,301	17,949	7.25	24,145	22,669
25.............	1,498	1,695	23,000	7.37	33,760	32,898
30.............	1,990	2,186	29,378	7.44	46,468	46,468
31.............	2,076	2,076	30,819	6.74	49,313	49,313
40.............	2,968	2,968	47,505	6.25	77,236	77,236
50.............	4,858	4,858	77,471	6.27	123,176	123,176
Ultimate..........	—	—	—	6.33	—	—

Contributions and benefits payable as of the beginning of each year.
Accrued Liability and Pension Fund calculated as of end of year, prior to contribution and benefit payments then due.
Initial Accrued Liability is 2,608.
Total Contributions for first 30 years includes amortization of Initial Accrued Liability of 196 per year.

TABLE 3A

Accrued Benefit Cost Method—Pro Rata Form (in thousands of dollars)

Year	Contribution Normal Cost	Contribution Total	Payroll	Total Contribution as % of Payroll	Accrued Liability	Pension Fund
1............	455	911	6,883	13.24%	6,848	975
2............	363	819	7,265	11.27	7,710	1,913
3...........	390	847	7,661	11.06	8,648	2,933
4...........	417	874	8,071	10.83	9,660	4,032
5...........	444	901	8,501	10.60	10,743	5,210
10...........	573	1,030	10,938	9.42	17,169	12,221
15...........	722	1,179	14,018	8.41	25,260	21,117
20...........	921	1,378	17,949	7.68	35,268	32,236
25...........	1,200	1,656	23,000	7.20	47,919	46,414
30...........	1,558	2,014	29,378	6.86	64,074	64,686
31...........	1,633	1,633	30,819	5.30	67,692	68,332
40...........	2,481	2,481	47,505	5.22	105,484	106,469
50...........	4,040	4,040	77,471	5.21	169,707	171,344
Ultimate.........	—	—	—	5.22	—	—

Contributions and benefits payable as of the beginning of each year.
Accrued Liability and Pension Fund calculated as of end of year, prior to contribution and benefit payments then due.
Initial Accrued Liability is 6,064.
Total Contribution for first 30 years includes amortization of Initial Accrued Liability of 457 per year.

TABLE 4A

Entry-Age Cost Method—Level Dollar Amount (in thousands of dollars)

Year	Contribution Normal Cost	Contribution Total	Payroll	Total Contribution as % of Payroll	Accrued Liability	Pension Fund
1............	354	975	6,883	14.17%	9,210	1,044
2............	366	988	7,265	13.60	10,240	2,167
3............	380	1,002	7,661	13.08	11,343	3,370
4............	395	1,017	8,071	12.60	12,519	4,653
5............	412	1,034	8,501	12.16	13,768	6,016
10............	514	1,136	10,938	10.39	21,104	14,056
15............	649	1,271	14,018	9.07	30,362	24,302
20............	824	1,445	17,949	8.05	41,869	37,192
25............	1,045	1,667	23,000	7.25	56,338	53,602
30............	1,335	1,957	29,378	6.66	74,583	74,583
31............	1,406	1,406	30,819	4.56	78,679	78,679
40............	2,209	2,209	47,505	4.65	122,511	122,511
50............	3,583	3,583	77,471	4.62	197,603	197,603
Ultimate.........	—	—	—	4.62	—	—

Contributions and benefits payable as of the beginning of each year.
Accrued Liability and Pension Fund calculated as of end of year, prior to contribution and benefit payments then due.
Initial Accrued Liability is 8,253.
Total Contribution for first 30 years includes amortization of Initial Accrued Liability of 621 per year.

TABLE 5A

Entry-Age Cost Method—Level Percent of Payroll (in thousands of dollars)

Year	Contribution Normal Cost	Contribution Total	Payroll	Total Contribution as % of Payroll	Accrued Liability	Pension Fund
1	347	860	6,883	12.49%	7,658	920
2	366	879	7,265	12.10	8,579	1,918
3	386	899	7,661	11.73	9,573	2,994
4	407	920	8,071	11.40	10,637	4,146
5	428	941	8,501	11.07	11,771	5,374
10	551	1,064	10,938	9.73	18,479	12,663
15	706	1,219	14,018	8.70	26,977	21,976
20	904	1,417	17,949	7.89	37,550	33,690
25	1,159	1,671	23,000	7.27	50,885	48,626
30	1,480	1,993	29,378	6.78	67,754	67,754
31	1,552	1,552	30,819	5.04	71,529	71,529
40	2,393	2,393	47,505	5.04	111,372	111,372
50	3,902	3,902	77,471	5.04	179,317	179,317
Ultimate	—	—	—	5.04	—	—

Contributions and benefits payable as of the beginning of each year.
Accrued Liability and Pension Fund calculated as of end of year, prior to contribution and benefit payments then due.
Initial Accrued Liability is 6,811.
Total Contribution for first 30 years includes amortization of Initial Accrued Liability of 513 per year.

TABLE 6A

Aggregate Cost Method—Original or Entry-Age Form (in thousands of dollars)

Year	Contribution	Payroll	Contribution as % of Payroll	Pension Fund
1	949	6,883	13.79%	1,015
2	954	7,265	13.13	2,100
3	960	7,661	12.53	3,255
4	967	8,071	11.98	4,477
5	976	8,501	11.48	5,765
10	1,036	10,938	9.47	13,201
15	1,134	14,018	8.09	22,355
20	1,281	17,949	7.14	33,516
25	1,490	23,000	6.48	47,383
30	1,769	29,378	6.02	64,733
31	1,833	30,819	5.95	68,596
40	2,606	47,505	5.49	109,103
50	4,064	77,471	5.25	177,598
Ultimate	—	—	5.04	—

Contributions and benefits payable as of the beginning of each year.
Pension Fund calculated as of end of year, prior to contribution and benefit payments then due.

TABLE 7A

Aggregate Cost Method—Accrued Benefit Form (in thousands of dollars)

Year	Contribution	Payroll	Contribution as % of Payroll	Pension Fund
1	418	6,883	6.07%	448
2	465	7,265	6.40	970
3	510	7,661	6.66	1,563
4	552	8,071	6.84	2,221
5	592	8,501	6.96	2,942
10	790	10,938	7.22	7,381
15	1,007	14,018	7.18	13,100
20	1,293	17,949	7.20	20,218
25	1,715	23,000	7.46	29,507
30	2,235	29,378	7.61	41,946
31	2,323	30,819	7.54	44,739
40	3,228	47,505	6.80	72,028
50	5,161	77,471	6.66	117,078
Ultimate	—	—	6.33	—

Contributions and benefits payable as of the beginning of each year.
Pension Fund calculated as of end of year, prior to contribution and benefit payments then due.

TABLE 8A

Frozen Initial Liability Method—Attained Age Normal Form (in thousands of dollars)

Year	Contribution Normal Cost	Contribution Total	Payroll	Contribution as % of Payroll	Pension Fund
1	718	915	6,883	13.29%	979
2	729	925	7,265	12.73	2,030
3	740	937	7,661	12.23	3,155
4	753	949	8,071	11.76	4,350
5	766	962	8,501	11.32	5,616
10	850	1,047	10,938	9.57	12,995
15	970	1,167	14,018	8.33	22,210
20	1,137	1,333	17,949	7.43	33,583
25	1,363	1,560	23,000	6.78	47,861
30	1,658	1,855	29,378	6.31	65,888
31	1,726	1,726	30,819	5.60	69,717
40	2,525	2,525	47,505	5.32	109,968
50	4,002	4,002	77,471	5.17	178,252
Ultimate	—	—	—	5.04	—

Contributions and benefits payable as of the beginning of each year.
Pension Fund calculated as of end of year, prior to contribution and benefit payments then due.
Initial Accrued Liability is 2,608.
Total contribution for first 30 years includes amortization of Initial Accrued Liability of 196 per year

TABLE 9A

Individual Level Funding—Level Percent of Payroll (in thousands of dollars)

Year	Contribution	Payroll	Contribution as % of Payroll	Pension Fund
1....................	1,228	6,883	17.84%	1,314
2....................	1,198	7,265	16.49	2,681
3....................	1,170	7,661	15.27	4,100
4....................	1,142	8,071	14.15	5,568
5....................	1,118	8,501	13.15	7,085
10....................	1,042	10,938	9.53	15,425
15....................	1,040	14,018	7.42	25,144
20....................	1,115	17,949	6.21	36,580
25....................	1,279	23,000	5.56	50,491
30....................	1,526	29,378	5.19	67,677
31....................	1,585	30,819	5.14	71,481
40....................	2,393	47,505	5.04	111,372
50....................	3,902	77,471	5.04	179,317
Ultimate..............	—	—	5.04	—

Contributions and benefits payable as of the beginning of each year.
Pension fund calculated as of end of year, prior to contribution and benefit payments then due.

TABLE 2B

Accrued Benefit Cost Method—Traditional Form (in thousands of dollars)

	Contribution			Total Contri-		
	Normal			bution as %	Accrued	Pension
Year	Cost	Total	Payroll	of Payroll	Liability	Fund
1.............	218	384	6,883	5.58%	2,264	419
2.............	247	413	7,265	5.68	2,731	900
3.............	276	442	7,661	5.77	3,257	1,442
4.............	303	469	8,071	5.81	3,838	2,041
5.............	329	495	8,501	5.82	4,471	2,694
10.............	456	622	10,938	5.69	8,354	6,702
15.............	599	765	14,018	5.46	13,327	11,868
20.............	789	955	17,949	5.32	19,470	18,308
25.............	1,082	1,248	23,000	5.43	27,435	26,731
30.............	1,454	1,620	29,378	5.51	38,134	38,134
31.............	1,517	1,517	30,819	4.92	40,542	40,542
40.............	2,143	2,143	47,505	4.51	63,846	63,846
50.............	3,504	3,504	77,471	4.52	101,635	101,635
Ultimate..........	—	—	—	4.57	—	—

Contributions and benefits payable as of the beginning of each year.
Accrued Liability and Pension Fund calculated as of end of year, prior to contribution and benefit payments then due.
Initial Accrued Liability is 1,859.
Total Contribution for first 30 years includes amortization of Initial Accrued Liability of 166 per year.

TABLE 3B

Accrued Benefit Cost Method—Pro Rata Form (in thousands of dollars)

| Year | Contribution | | Payroll | Total Contribution as % of Payroll | Accrued Liability | Pension Fund |
	Normal Cost	Total				
1.............	271	633	6,883	9.20%	4,626	689
2.............	210	571	7,265	7.86	5,267	1,368
3.............	227	589	7,661	7.69	5,971	2,112
4.............	245	606	8,071	7.51	6,736	2,921
5.............	262	623	8,501	7.33	7,559	3,793
10.............	343	704	10,938	6.44	12,513	9,064
15.............	434	796	14,018	5.68	18,823	15,848
20.............	555	917	17,949	5.11	26,662	24,397
25.............	731	1,092	23,000	4.75	36,652	35,451
30.............	957	1,319	29,378	4.49	49,572	49,978
31.............	1,003	1,003	30,819	3.25	52,467	52,891
40.............	1,501	1,501	47,505	3.16	82,070	82,722
50.............	2,447	2,447	77,471	3.16	131,649	132,730
Ultimate..........	—	—	—	3.17	—	—

Contributions and benefits payable as of the beginning of each year.
Accrued Liability and Pension Fund calculated as of end of year, prior to contribution and benefit payments then due.
Initial Accrued Liability is 4,050.
Total Contribution for first 30 years includes amortization of Initial Accrued Liability of 362 per year.

TABLE 4B

Entry-Age Cost Method—Level Dollar Amount (in thousands of dollars)

| Year | Contribution | | Payroll | Total Contribution as % of Payroll | Accrued Liability | Pension Fund |
	Normal Cost	Total				
1.............	180	673	6,883	9.78%	6,218	734
2.............	186	680	7,265	9.36	6,974	1,534
3.............	193	687	7,661	8.97	7,792	2,400
4.............	201	695	8,071	8.61	8,671	3,331
5.............	210	703	8,501	8.27	9,610	4,328
10.............	262	755	10,938	6.90	15,198	10,288
15.............	331	824	14,018	5.88	22,320	17,984
20.............	419	913	17,949	5.09	31,211	27,756
25.............	532	1,025	23,000	4.46	42,481	40,381
30.............	680	1,173	29,378	3.99	56,833	56,833
31.............	715	715	30,819	2.32	60,049	60,049
40.............	1,124	1,124	47,505	2.37	93,764	93,764
50.............	1,824	1,824	77,471	2.35	150,824	150,824
Ultimate..........	—	—	—	2.35	—	—

Contributions and benefits payable as of the beginning of each year.
Accrued Liability and Pension Fund calculated as of end of year, prior to contribution and benefit payments then due.
Initial Accrued Liability is 5,525.
Total Contribution for first 30 years includes amortization of Initial Accrued Liability of 493 per year.

TABLE 5B

Entry-Age Cost Method—Level Percent of Payroll (in thousands of dollars)

Year	Contribution Normal Cost	Contribution Total	Payroll	Total Contribution as % of Payroll	Accrued Liability	Pension Fund
1............	189	620	6,883	9.01%	5,464	676
2............	200	631	7,265	8.69	6,167	1,417
3............	211	642	7,661	8.38	6,932	2,224
4............	222	653	8,071	8.09	7,756	3,094
5............	234	665	8,501	7.82	8,639	4,027
10............	301	732	10,938	6.69	13,919	9,632
15............	386	817	14,018	5.83	20,667	16,881
20............	494	925	17,949	5.15	29,098	26,080
25............	633	1,064	23,000	4.63	39,810	37,975
30............	809	1,239	29,378	4.22	53,490	53,490
31............	848	848	30,819	2.75	56,551	56,551
40............	1,308	1,308	47,505	2.75	88,322	88,322
50............	2,132	2,132	77,471	2.75	141,888	141,888
Ultimate..........	—	—	—	2.75	—	—

Contributions and benefits payable as of the beginning of each year.
Accrued Liability and Pension Fund calculated as of end of year, prior to contribution and benefit payments then due.
Initial Accrued Liability is 4,824.
Total Contribution for first 30 years includes amortization of Initial Accrued Liability of 431 per year.

TABLE 6B

Aggregate Cost Method—Original or Entry-Age Form (in thousands of dollars)

Year	Contribution	Payroll	Contribution as % of Payroll	Pension Fund
1....................	689	6,883	10.01%	751
2....................	688	7,265	9.47	1,561
3....................	688	7,661	8.98	2,432
4....................	689	8,071	8.54	3,360
5....................	691	8,501	8.13	4,345
10....................	709	10,938	6.48	10,108
15....................	749	14,018	5.34	17,296
20....................	816	17,949	4.55	26,124
25....................	920	23,000	4.00	37,201
30....................	1,061	29,378	3.61	51,219
31....................	1,094	30,819	3.55	54,343
40....................	1,497	47,505	3.15	86,586
50....................	2,279	77,471	2.94	140,547
Ultimate................	—	—	2.75	—

Contributions and benefits payable as of the beginning of each year.
Pension Fund calculated as of end of year, prior to contribution and benefit payments then due.

TABLE 7B

Aggregate Cost Method—Accrued Benefit Form (in thousands of dollars)

Year	Contribution	Payroll	Contribution as % of Payroll	Pension Fund
1...	303	6,883	4.40%	330
2...	341	7,265	4.69	724
3...	377	7,661	4.92	1,179
4...	411	8,071	5.09	1,691
5...	443	8,501	5.21	2,256
10...	596	10,938	5.45	5,789
15...	760	14,018	5.42	10,374
20...	978	17,949	5.45	16,076
25...	1,311	23,000	5.70	23,586
30...	1,729	29,378	5.89	33,884
31...	1,795	30,819	5.82	36,212
40...	2,454	47,505	5.17	58,554
50...	3,899	77,471	5.03	94,894
Ultimate...	—	—	4.57	—

Contributions and benefits payable as of the beginning of each year.
Pension Fund calculated as of end of year, prior to contribution and benefit payments then due.

TABLE 8B

Frozen Initial Liability Method—Attained Age Normal Form (in thousands of dollars)

Year	Contribution Normal Cost	Total	Payroll	Contribution as % of Payroll	Pension Fund
1...	496	662	6,883	9.62%	722
2...	500	666	7,265	9.17	1,506
3...	504	670	7,661	8.75	2,352
4...	509	675	8,071	8.36	3,257
5...	515	681	8,501	8.01	4,222
10...	552	718	10,938	6.56	9,925
15...	609	775	14,018	5.53	17,136
20...	692	858	17,949	4.78	26,108
25...	809	975	23,000	4.24	37,502
30...	964	1,130	29,378	3.85	52,093
31...	999	999	30,819	3.24	55,192
40...	1,424	1,424	47,505	3.00	87,253
50...	2,223	2,223	77,471	2.87	141,060
Ultimate...	—	—	—	2.75	—

Contributions and benefits payable as of the beginning of each year.
Accrued Liability and Pension Fund calculated as of end of year, prior to contribution and benefit payments then due.
Initial Accrued Liability is 1,859.
Total Contribution for first 30 years includes amortization of Initial Accrued Liability of 166 per year.

TABLE 9B

Individual Level Funding—Level Percent of Payroll (in thousands of dollars)

Year	Contribution	Payroll	Contribution as % of Payroll	Pension Fund
1....................	903	6,883	13.12%	985
2....................	871	7,265	11.99	2,015
3....................	840	7,661	10.96	3,092
4....................	810	8,071	10.04	4,211
5....................	782	8,501	9.20	5,373
10....................	681	10,938	6.23	11,823
15....................	636	14,018	4.54	19,425
20....................	648	17,949	3.61	28,445
25....................	719	23,000	3.13	39,543
30....................	840	29,378	2.86	53,433
31....................	870	30,819	2.82	56,512
40....................	1,308	47,505	2.75	88,322
50....................	2,132	77,471	2.75	141,888
Ultimate................	—	—	2.75	—

Contributions and benefits payable as of the beginning of each year.
Pension fund calculated as of end of year, prior to contribution and benefit payments then due.

14

Ancillary Benefits

THE PENSION FUNDING problem in its simplest form involves a retirement benefit only. However, in many plans other events give rise to benefits. Benefits payable upon death or disability, and lump sum benefits payable upon termination of employment, are sometimes called ancillary benefits, when viewed in the context of a pension plan. Retirement benefits payable to vested terminators are considered by the authors to be part and parcel of the basic pension benefit, and are not included among the ancillary benefits to which this chapter is addressed.

Because the contributions required to fund ancillary benefits are not normally a significant proportion of the total contributions, and because the theoretically exact formulae for valuing ancillary benefits are sometimes difficult, approximate methods are rather commonly employed.

DEATH BENEFITS

There are several different kinds of death (or survivor) benefits commonly associated with defined benefit pension plans. Each will be discussed separately.

The Joint and Survivor Option

A common option provided by pension plans of the past, one that must be offered a married worker under the 1974 pension legislation, is the right of a pensioner to receive a reduced pension, all or some of which is continued through the lifetime of a named co-annuitant. The co-annuitant will usually, but not necessarily, be the pensioner's spouse, the option being designed to fit the pension needs of a couple, rather than the worker alone. There may or may not be a reduction in pension upon the death of the spouse, if there is a reduction upon the death of the pensioner. The option must be elected at (or sometimes prior to) retirement date, and once elected usually cannot be revoked. Under ERISA the joint and survivor form is automatic, and specific action is required to elect any other forms.

These options will not give rise to any special pension funding problems, or indeed to any additional contributions to the pension arrangement, *if* the reduced pension is calculated on the principle of actuarial equivalence. This principle requires that the present values at retirement date, of the normal form pension and the joint and survivor form, be equal. To establish this equivalence assumptions are needed as to rates of mortality by age and sex, and as to the rate of investment earnings. Usually the valuation assumptions as to these factors are employed.

Should any of the joint and survivor options be calculated on a principle other than that of actuarial equivalence, or should the equivalence be based on other than the valuation assumptions, then the rate of election of the options will theoretically enter into the pension funding calculations. An actuarial basis for the joint and survivor option that is biased toward the election of the option clearly adds to the cost of the pension plan.

There is some reason to believe that even an actuarially equivalent option adds to pension plan costs, if the option can be elected or rejected as late as the actual retirement date. (21) Retirees then in good health are presumed to elect the straight life annuity form, while those in not such good health may have a tendency to accept the optional form. Some actuaries reflect this tendency toward anti-selection by treating participants as younger than they actually are, or counter it through plan design by a requirement of earlier election.

Postretirement Death Benefits

Pension plans occasionally guarantee that the pension will continue for at least n months, where n is some arbitrary number such as 60 or 120. In contributory plans it is common to provide a post-retirement death benefit of the excess of employee contributions (often with interest at some specified rate to retirement date) over the pension payments made.

Postretirement death benefits can be taken into account in the calculation of the present value of pension benefits at retirement. Five or ten-year guarantees on the duration of the pension cause no particular complication, since the formulae are relatively simple. The adjustment for postretirement death benefits based on the guarantee of return of contributions is more complicated, but well within the abilities of the qualified pension actuary.

If postretirement death benefits are provided only as optional forms, with the principle of actuarial equivalence operating, the option can generally be ignored in the pension calculations. The previous discussion with respect to the joint and survivor form is generally applicable.

The Preretirement Spouse Pension

Some pension plans pay a pension to a surviving spouse when the worker dies prior to retirement. The amount of the pension is likely to be in some way related to the pension that the worker had earned prior to death. It may be designed to reproduce the spouse pension that would have been payable had the worker died after retiring early with a joint and survivor election in effect. The spouse pension may or may not be terminated if the surviving spouse remarries.

Spouse pensions can be funded in the same manner as the basic pension benefit, though additional assumptions as to the probability of there being a surviving spouse when the employee dies, and of subsequent remarriage of such spouse, are needed. (11) This is a complicated approach, however, and simpler methods are perhaps as satisfactory.

Funding of preretirement spouse pensions on what in life insurance terms is called a one-year term basis will usually work out well. In event of plan termination spouse pensions already in course of payment will be funded; and, while the budgeting characteristics of such funding are not ideal, this benefit is not likely to represent a significant proportion of the value of total benefits.

The preretirement spouse pension may not be an additional benefit, but may instead be an optional benefit paid for by the worker by his acceptance of a reduced pension. As long as the principle of actuarial equivalence applies, this option, like the other options previously noted, can be ignored in the funding calculations.

RETURN OF CONTRIBUTIONS
ON DEATH OR WITHDRAWAL

Upon death or withdrawal of an employee under a contributory pension plan, he or his beneficiary is usually entitled to the return of any contributions he has made to the pension fund, often with interest thereon at a specified rate. If this lump sum death or withdrawal benefit has not been taken into account in the normal valuation of the retirement benefits, additional contributions are required.

The best theoretical approach is to include these benefits with the basic retirement benefit, and to use consistent actuarial cost methods throughout. This is not at all convenient, however; and there are at least two less theoretically correct but possibly more practical ways of recognizing the return-of-employee-contributions feature of contributory plans prior to retirement. The handling of the postretirement death benefit arising from employee contributions has been mentioned earlier.

One approach is the funding, at the time each employee contribution is made, of the present value of the lump sum death or withdrawal benefit arising therefrom. This present value takes the form of a single premium for an increasing death or withdrawal payment for the remaining years to retirement. To recognize the "with interest" feature, the valuation interest rate prior to retirement can be reduced by the interest rate allowed in calculating the lump sum benefit. This procedure has similarities with the accrued benefit method of funding retirement benefits, and is rather a natural way of funding return-of-contribution benefits when the accrued benefit methods are employed.

A second approach is perhaps more natural for entry-age cost methods. Employee contributions are less effective in funding retirement benefits than the employer contribution, because the latter accumulate "with benefit of survivorship" while the former are returned with interest when the employee leaves the active group prior to retirement. Recognizing this, the normal employer contribution for year y for persons age x can be increased by

$$(1 - {}_{r-x}p_x)E_x$$

where E_x represents the y year employee contributions at age x, and ${}_{r-x}p_x$ is the probability of a worker age x surviving in active employment until retirement. The approximation involved is slightly conservative if the valuation rate of interest exceeds the rate at which employee contributions accumulate.

DISABILITY BENEFITS

Perhaps a majority of long-term disability plans for employees are independent of the pension arrangements for those employees. When this is true, any provisions with respect to disability are outside of the pension funding problem.

There are nonetheless important pension plans (including U.S. Social Security) where retirement due to age and retirement due to disability are viewed as two facets of the more general income replacement problem, and the disability benefit is viewed as a second form of pension. Where old-age and disability pensions are paid through the same arrangements and use the same fund, disability benefits clearly become an ancillary benefit for which funding must be provided.

Although it is technically possible to apply the actuarial cost methods devised for retirement situations to disability benefits, many actuaries see little advantage in doing so. Instead the one-year term technique is often employed. This technique, adapted from group long-term disability insurance, often has generally satisfactory characteristics when the disability benefit is a part of a pension plan. From an employee security viewpoint, disability benefits are funded as soon as disability is proved, and a terminating plan can therefore preserve disability pensions already in course of payment. There may be rising cost characteristics to this type of funding; however, it is usually felt that these will seldom be of enough magnitude to cause concern.

Actuaries that prefer to include the disability benefit as a part of the basic calculations, thereby funding this benefit by the same actuarial cost method as is used for the retirement benefit, sometimes do so in an approximate manner, recognizing thereby that the knowledge of disability incidence rates, and the rates of death or recovery by those disabled, leaves much to be desired. A simple percentage addition to the contributions otherwise calculated has sometimes proved to be fairly satisfactory.

OTHER ANCILLARY BENEFITS

This work treats pure retirement benefits as a part of the mainstream of pension funding, even though complications may arise from early or late retirement, or from vested terminations. It treats death, disability, or cash withdrawal benefits as ancillary benefits.

Occasionally one finds a defined-benefit pension plan granting a lump sum at retirement in lieu of the monthly income otherwise payable. Whether this benefit is viewed as a part of the regular retirement picture, or as an ancillary benefit of the cash withdrawal type, is essentially immaterial. The section on postretirement death benefits earlier in this chapter applies, particularly the discussion of actuarial equivalence and of potential antiselection.

Although this discussion of ancillary benefits seems to cover the benefits that are common in defined-benefit pension arrangements, a very few pension plans may provide unemployment benefits, for example; or preretirement children's benefits. The actuary needs to be alert to any unusual provision with a cost impact.

15

Difficult Practical Problems

THE PENSION FUNDING problem is not a simple one, and complications can arise from any one of several sources. This chapter discusses several matters which give particular difficulty. Generally acceptable solutions to some aspects of these problems have not yet been developed.

THE INTEGRATED PLAN

Many defined-benefit pension plans have benefit formulae designed to be "integrated" with U.S. Social Security. It is intended that the total pension benefit at retirement, including the Social Security old age benefit, bear a reasonable relationship to the covered worker's salary or wage and his years of covered service.

The technical problem of satisfactory integration by good design of the private plan benefit formula has proved to be a difficult one. The old-age benefit under Social Security has quite different characteristics than the typical private pension plan, recognizing covered service to a lesser degree and marital status more. Social Security benefits now have built-in cost-of-living adjustments (not a feature of the majority of private pension plans); and the taxable earnings base, upon which the Social Security benefit for high paid workers is based, is also dynamic, increasing automatically in step with per-worker earnings in covered employment. The base has increased very rapidly in the recent past—reaching $15,300 in 1976 while it was only $7,800 as recently as 1970. The problems of successful benefit design incorporating the integration principle are made worse by the very complicated IRS regulations (in 1976 badly out of date) intended to avoid discrimination in favor of the highly paid.

Attempts to integrate private pensions with Social Security seem to fall into two general classes: (1) those *directly integrated* (sometimes called "offset") plans that define a total benefit, then subtract or offset some portion of the Social Security benefit, and (2) those that provide larger benefits on that part of salary earnings above a "break-point" (related to the Social Security taxable earnings base) to adjust for a Social Security benefit which ignores such earnings.

These benefit design problems are not within the scope of this work, but the funding problems arising from efforts to integrate the benefit formulae of private pensions are worthy of mention. One matter posing difficulty is that integrated plans are characteristically more subject to inflationary forces than plans that are unintegrated, because the slope of the pension earned in any year (from the employer's plan) may be steeper. The "leverage" of the subtractive social security element makes the funding of integrated plans treacherous, particularly under the accrued benefit cost methods.

Special problems that arise under offset plans include (1) the necessity of estimating the offsetting Social Security benefit for workers retiring in different calendar years, with partially unknown Social Security wage records, and under a dynamic Social Security law, and (2) the allocation of the Social Security benefit to a particular year, for purposes of determining benefits for vested quits, or for application of the accrued benefit cost methods. The allocation problem is not so crucial under projected benefit cost methods, but it may arise even here where the employee's working career is not entirely with the employer sponsoring the plan in question.

Under the second approach to integration the problems are of a somewhat different nature, but probably at least as difficult. Here the level at which the formula breaks is the troublesome element. Though the benefit formula may seem to establish where the break-point will be in the somewhat distant future, common sense requires that the point rise as the taxable earnings base for Social Security rises. The problem of allocation to a particular year of service, essential to the accrued benefit cost method, remains.

THE FIXED BENEFIT—FIXED CONTRIBUTION PLAN

By the very nature of the pension funding problem, plans of the defined-contribution (money purchase) type are excluded, and plans of the defined-benefit type included. These two types are usually thought of as mutually exclusive, and as a matter of fact usually are.

There is, however, a type of defined-benefit plan that seems to have fixed the contribution schedule as well as the benefit formula. Such a fixed benefit-fixed contribution plan is a logical impossibility over the long run. This is clear from a study of Figure 2 on page 7. If the flows through both the inlet and outlet valves are determined by forces over which the system managers have no control, there is no means of adjustment for experience gain or loss that is bound to occur, and the fund level must absorb whichever actually occurs. Eventually the reservoir will either run dry or overflow. Periodic renegotiation of benefits and contributions may alleviate the problem to some degree.

Should the actuarial assumptions on which the original equivalence of contributions and benefits was based prove to be conservative, the fund will grow beyond the accrued liability for the benefits promised. Eventually the overfunding will become obvious, and pressures will build for a reduction in contributions, or, more likely, an increase in benefits. Either the fixed benefit or the fixed contribution must give—or both must. In the case of conservative assumptions examined here at least there is "good news" for someone, and no really serious problems occur.

In the reverse situation, the actuarial assumptions prove to be overly optimistic, and after a few years signs of underfunding appear. Here pressure from the employer side will make very difficult an increase in contributions, yet resistance to a cut in benefits will be as strong or stronger. The tendency will be toward inertia, letting the situation get even worse. The consequences of underfunding are "bad news" for one or the other (or both) of employer or employee, and are considerably more serious than the consequences of over-conservatism.

The reaction of the pension actuary to the potential future difficulties of a pension plan attempting to fix both contributions and benefits is likely to take two forms. First he would like to avoid the problem by leaving the contribution level open. If it is clear to all parties concerned that contributions may have to be adjusted in the future, and that the only real commitment is to the benefit side (even though there may be an understanding that contributions for a short period are set at some particular level), the potential problem largely disappears. Failing such an agreement, however, the natural reaction of the actuary is to build enough conservatism into the actuarial cost method, or into the actuarial assumptions, that the probability of future underfunding is low.

It is unfortunate, but true, that situations will arise where neither of these ways of avoiding future problems is possible. Parties to the negotiations setting up a plan, or modifying a plan already in being, may well insist on fixing both contributions and benefits, and on leaving vague the means of keeping the two in balance. To make things worse, there is a natural pressure from the employee side toward optimistic assumptions and unconservative techniques, since representatives of employees want to get benefits as high as possible. Although in the bargaining process the employer may be trying to increase the apparent cost of benefits negotiated, once the bargaining is over he too may like the thin funding that optimistic assumptions seem to justify. Short range considerations are likely to dominate the long range, and the actuary may well find himself out of rapport with his clientele if he takes too conservative a position. There have been cases, and there will be again, where the actuary's position as actuarial advisor to a plan may depend on his satisfying short range considerations at the expense of the long term health of the funding arrangements.

THE MULTIPLE EMPLOYER PLAN

Multiple employer plans of the Taft-Hartley type have special characteristics that may give rise to difficult funding problems.

1. There are often large numbers of small employers, not all of whom join the plan at the same time.
2. There is likely to be a larger than usual amount of noncontinuous employment, and many persons with partial service credits. There may well be reciprocity arrangements whereby service with another employer counts.
3. The initial data as to age and amount of past service of the employees of the many employers may be inaccurate or unavailable; and there may be considerable uncertainty as to what employers will eventually be included.

4. Another actuarial assumption, the average number of hours worked per year, may be needed—and when contributions are directly related to hours worked, and benefits promised less so, this assumption may be critical.
5. There may well be questions as to pooling of experience. It is not obvious that each group is willing to be pooled with the others, particularly with respect to how much accrued liability each group is responsible for. If one or more employers later choose to withdraw from the pooled arrangement, an equitable settlement is difficult.
6. Finally, this type of plan is especially likely to fix both contributions (expressed as ¢ per hour or % of payroll) and benefits, and hence give rise to the misunderstandings and possible underfunding suggested earlier.

Actuarial valuation work for multiple employer plans is something of a specialty within a specialty, and is not an easy area for the inexperienced.

THE VERY SMALL PLAN

Plans with only a handful of employees, or somewhat larger plans with a preponderance of the benefits concentrated in a very few, present difficulties in the appropriate choice of actuarial assumptions. The actual experience as to mortality, withdrawal, and salary increase may be entirely dominated by what happens to the highest paid individual. In a fully insured plan there may be a third-party guarantee with respect to the mortality and interest elements.

In the absence of such guarantees, the most conservative of assumptions are in order. Assumptions of no mortality and no employee withdrawal are not uncommon, may be considered the most likely, and are probably called for in very small plans or those where one or two individuals dominate. Such an approach may, however, run afoul of IRS rules—or some of the provisions of ERISA—especially if death or withdrawal of a highly paid employee results in the plan becoming "overfunded."

THE WHOLE LIFE AND SIDE FUND ARRANGEMENT

Pension plans using individual life insurance policies or annuities as a funding vehicle pose no difficult funding problems provided such policies are used exclusively. The individual level premium cost method is natural to individual level premium life insurance of the retirement endowment type, or to the individual retirement annuity. There is no unfunded accrued liability to be concerned with, the level contribution with respect to each individual participant is rather easily determined, and actuarial gains which arise from the use of very conservative assumptions show up as dividends paid by the insurer or as employer credits arising from nonvested termination.

Individual policy pension trusts more recently entered into tend, however, to use the lower premium whole life form of individual policy, supplemented by an unallocated side fund. Under this arrangement the level premium life insurance policy provides a pre-retirement lump sum death benefit (which is typically $1,000 of life insurance for each $10 of prospective pension), and the cash value of the policy at retirement is enough to provide some fraction (usually around $\frac{1}{3}$) of the pension, through use of the settlement options the policy contains. The remaining pension comes from application of a part of the side fund to buy additional annuity.

This more complicated arrangement, using individually issued whole life policies (or occasionally group permanent contracts on the whole life plan) and an unallocated side fund, is considerably more difficult from a pension funding point of view. These difficulties are not made easier by the fact that most plans using this arrangement include very few employees, so that the special difficulties of the very small plan are also involved. There are two general approaches.

One of these calculates, on a participant-by-participant basis, the amount of pension at retirement provided by the life insurance policy's cash value, subtracts this amount from the prospective pension, and funds the remainder separately. The total contribution becomes (1) the premium less dividends on the life insurance policies, adjusted for cash values released by nonvested termination, plus (2) the normal cost for the side fund, plus (3) the contribution toward the accrued liability, if any, on the side fund portion.

When additional whole life coverage is issued due to change in compensation level, the premium level is increased. The side fund is thus relieved of a part of its obligations; and if all experience was in accordance with the assumptions there would be an actuarial gain. More likely, salary increases were not anticipated in the side fund funding calculation, and the overall effect is an actuarial loss.

To reduce the complications of the first described approach, some actuaries prefer to calculate the contributions for the entirety of the pension and insurance benefits by means of whatever actuarial cost method and actuarial assumptions they think most appropriate; then consider the payment to the life insurance carrier as one portion of that contribution, with the remainder flowing into the side fund. In years after the first the cash values of the insurance policies must be added to the side fund to calculate plan assets, but otherwise the funding is being handled almost as if the individual policies did not exist. Care must be taken that the rather high level of expense is recognized, and that the interest earnings rate assumed recognizes that some of the assets are insurance policy cash values.

Neither of the above solutions is ideal, because either may involve a confounding of actuarial cost methods and inconsistent sets of actuarial assumptions. Handling of the vesting provisions required by ERISA will be troublesome as well, since the different vesting requirements that apply to plans wholly funded by individual policies do not apply to the whole life and side fund vehicle.

16

The Regulatory Environment

MANY PRACTICES in the business world are directly affected by law or regulation, or indirectly affected by federal income tax considerations. Accounting practices are influenced by the views of the accounting profession, particularly when an audited financial statement is required by a governmental regulatory body. Pension funding is no exception to these general statements. The practices in this area have grown out of a regulatory environment which was originally confined largely to certain sections of the Internal Revenue Code and its supporting regulations; but which has expanded to include principles established by the accounting profession, and more recently comprehensive pension legislation at the federal level.

The pension actuary must recognize the regulatory environment in which his client finds himself. The compliance requirements on the employer in the private sector have become so great that they tend to dwarf more general considerations. Although the strictly legalistic view of pension funding is far too narrow, the regulatory environment is of great importance, and cannot be ignored. References to this environment have occasionally been made in preceding chapters, but the subject has largely been left to this one.

This chapter is a description of the ways in which the pension funding problem is affected by the legal and accounting framework under which private pension plans operate. No attempt will be made to cover the laws and regulations in all detail, even as to those parts directly impinging upon the matters to which this volume is directed. It would clearly be a mistake for the pension actuary to rely on this volume to convey all he may need to know about the regulatory environment. More detailed coverage of the ERISA legislation, in particular, will be found elsewhere. (31)

Those matters that the authors consider the most important features of the regulatory environment, as it affects the problem of pension funding, will be covered. The initial emphasis will be on the implications of the Internal Revenue Code, as it developed over the period from about 1940 to the passage of the ERISA legislation in 1974. The effect of "generally accepted accounting principles" as they developed for pension plans in the mid-60s will then be explored. (27) Finally, the changes brought about by the 1974 legislation will be examined, recognizing, however, that the full impact of ERISA will not be known for some time. In the discussion of all three, the authors will emphasize what the regulators were trying to accomplish, with perhaps less emphasis on their means of doing so.

THE INTERNAL REVENUE CODE AND IRS REGULATIONS— PRIOR TO 1974

The history of the Internal Revenue Code and its supporting regulatory framework evidences two particular concerns about pension funding.

One had to do with the potential loss in tax revenues if an employer were permitted to fund his pension plan without limit, getting an income tax deduction in his corporate return for the heavy contributions made. The fact that interest earned within the qualified pension trust was nontaxable, and that the beneficiaries paid income tax only on amounts actually received in the form of benefits, added to the government's concern. Although there is substantial question whether the tax treatment of qualified pension plans amounts in the long run to a subsidization of such plans, it is clear that employers can reduce their immediate tax liability by heavy funding. The so-called "maximum" rules for deductible contributions were established to prevent the deduction in any one year of more than the Treasury considered a reasonable amount.

The second concern had to do with the requirements that a qualified plan be permanent in nature, and not discriminate in favor of the highly paid. It was felt that a plan might be set up to provide for a few executives at or near retirement, then terminate before the rank and file ever became entitled to retirement benefits. To avoid a discrimination in favor of the highly paid, Mimeograph 5717 provided that benefits for the 25 highest paid plan participants were to be cut back, in event of a plan termination within 10 years or failure to meet certain funding requirements. Except for the possible effect on the highly paid, there was little penalty for under-funding. There were some minimum funding requirements as to multi-employer plans, and as to negotiated plans where the bargaining agreement had a fixed termination date—but with these exceptions a plan did not really need to meet any minimum funding standards to achieve a qualified status.

Maximum Deductible Contribution

In establishing that the plan contribution in any year was fully deductible under the maximum deductible contribution rules, an employer had three different tests that could be applied.

The first test let the employer deduct up to 5 percent of covered compensation without an actuarial showing of any kind.

The second established rules for the aggregate and individual level premium cost methods. Neither of these methods include an initial accrued liability. Contributions thereunder were fully deductible, subject to proper adjustment for actuarial gain; and, in the case of the individual level premium form, to the initial weighted average years of funding being not less than five years.

The third test was that most frequently employed, because it was directly applicable to the accrued benefit and entry-age cost methods, then as now the methods in most common use. Under either method the maximum deductible contribution in any year was defined as the normal cost, plus 10 percent of a "past service base," less an adjustment for any experience gains. The base was essentially the initial accrued liability under the actuarial cost method employed, plus any increase in accrued liability resulting from later plan amendment or from failure to meet the normal cost, plus any past experience loss not offset by experience gains. The resulting maximum deductible contribution was normally higher when the entry-age cost method was in use than under the accrued benefit cost method, because of the similarity of the rule and the higher level of conservatism under the entry-age method.

The maximum deductible contribution under this third test was reduced to the normal cost, less an adjustment for experience gains, once the accrued liability under the method chosen had been fully funded.

Aside from the possible nondeductibility of a part of a particular year's contribution, there was no real bar under IRS rules to very conservative funding of a pension plan. A contribution not deductible in any year could be carried over to be deducted later, and employers occasionally funded initial accrued liabilities very rapidly to achieve quickly a high degree of employee security. The IRS sometimes balked at specific actuarial assumptions it felt unreasonable; but all in all a plan could be funded rather rapidly if that were desired. Employers not subject to income tax had no restriction of any kind.

Minimum Funding Requirements

The test of whether a partial plan termination might have occurred was based on an accumulative test, not on a year-to-year one. Under either the accrued benefit or entry-age cost methods, it was enough to show that the unfunded accrued liability as of valuation date was no greater than the sum of the initial accrued liability and any accrued liability resulting from later plan amendment.

Initially the minimum funding level necessary to meet the test was therefore the sum of the normal cost and interest at the valuation rate on the initial accrued liability; but any funding in excess of this amount directly reduced the requirement for later years. After a plan had operated for a time with some funding of the initial accrued liability, the employer contribution could drop to zero without risk of benefit reduction on the highest paid. Unfunding of a partially funded accrued liability was permissible because protection of employee pension expectations was not one of the law's objectives. Avoidance of discrimination in favor of the highly paid was the main intent.

General Situation under Pre-1974 IRS Rules

Other than meeting the maximum funding requirements, and what little requirement there was as to minimum funding, the employer had really no restriction upon the manner chosen to fund the pension plan. The employer enjoyed great flexibility, being able to make large contributions when profits were high (and thereby reducing reported profits) and little or no contribution when profits were missing or small (thereby increasing the reported profit). The popularity of the with-supplemental-liability forms of actuarial cost methods stemmed at least partially from the flexibility offered by the initial accrued liability and by the possibility of varying its amortization depending upon management objectives. Some criticism was leveled at the opportunity offered to manage profit by control over the employer contribution (especially for labor intensive industry where profits were very sensitive to wages paid, and hence to pension contributions), but there were no real bars to such practice.

There were certain other characteristics of the legal framework that some technicians viewed as less than completely satisfactory.

1. The degree of conservatism employed by the pension actuary in making a choice of actuarial cost methods and actuarial assumptions greatly affected both the maximum and any minimum funding levels. The more conservatism employed, the higher both of these levels become. The actuary's professional judgment and the need of the employer to justify the plan contribution were at least occasionally in conflict. The IRS, knowing this, was not surprisingly suspicious, especially of assumptions that appeared to them to be over-conservative.
2. The maximum deductible contribution limitations quite possibly had the effect of reducing the general level of funding below what it might otherwise have been, and thus a negative effect on the security of pension expectations.
3. The protection seemingly afforded to employees against badly underfunded plans was more apparent than real. IRS regulations have never acted as a bar to the most underfunded plans of all—the pay-as-you-go type. Whereas pay-as-you-go plans were seldom qualified under the rules, these plans had satisfactory tax treatment even though unqualified, and there was little reason to qualify them.
4. Certain technical problems were never satisfactorily solved. The IRS rules did not apply at all well to actuarial cost methods of the individual level premium type, and the necessary modifications were cumbersome and not particularly equitable. More-

over, the rules regarding adjustments for actuarial gain and loss were loosely indicated at best.

Despite what some technicians viewed as an IRS bias against well funded plans, investigations of funding status in the mid-60s concluded that, in the overall, plans in existence for as long as ten years were fairly well funded. (19)

GENERALLY ACCEPTED ACCOUNTING PRINCIPLES

As early as 1948 the American Institute of Certified Public Accountants became interested in the proper accounting for pension plans. Their early efforts were largely with respect to the handling of "past service costs," by which was meant the "initial accrued liability" in the terminology of this volume. Accounting Research Bulletins 36, 43, and 47 made it clear that past service costs should be charged against the present and future periods. ARB 47, issued in 1956, was the most specific, saying that "costs based on past services should be charged off over some reasonable period, provided the allocation is made on a systematic and rational basis and does not cause distortion of the operating results in any one year."

Until the mid-60s the CPAs had no position more definite than ARB 47 against the charging of pension costs exactly as these were funded, even though the funding might vary widely from year to year, and could as a consequence have a material effect on reported earnings.

After an extensive investigation, to which the actuarial profession had considerable input, the Accounting Principles Board published a report of their study, (26) an exposure draft of their proposed guideline to CPA's (June, 1966), and finally APB *Opinion No. 8*, (27) an opinion which established "generally accepted accounting principles" for corporate pension plans.

It is not surprising that APB 8 looks for a good solution to the budgeting problem and is not particularly concerned with the companion problem, that related to the security of employee expectations. From the accountant's standpoint, the problem is solved when an appropriate provision is made on the company books, whether or not the same amount is contributed to a segregated trust fund. If the recommended expense charge is different from the amount actually contributed, then the CPA expects an asset or liability adjustment on the corporate books to effectively change the cash contributed to what the accountant views as an appropriate accrual.

The ideal expense charge from the accountant's viewpoint would be that charge most nearly level (in absolute dollars, in dollars per active participant, or better yet as a percent of payroll) and most readily recognizable as attributable to work performed during the accounting period. Any payment toward the unfunded accrued liability, particularly if that payment is viewed as attributable to work performed in some earlier time period, leaves something to be desired from the accountant's viewpoint.

Probably because accountants realize there is no perfect solution, and that there was difference of opinion as to how pension expense could best be charged, APB 8 in effect recommends a charge to operations within a range. The recommended charge is equal to the normal cost, plus a percentage of the initial accrued liability, plus the same percentage of any additional accrued liability arising from past plan liberalizations, with an adjustment for actuarial gain or loss. The percentage can be set at any level, so long as it is uniformly applied, and so long as the resulting charge neither exceeds a maximum or is less than a minimum.

The maximum accrual or charge is essentially the same as the maximum deductible amount under IRS regulations, as these stood in 1966 when APB 8 was issued. The most important exception pertains to those plans whose accrual differs from the amount funded. If the past accrual has been greater than the amount funded, a balance sheet liability has been set up to make up for the missing funding, and interest at the valuation rate on the liability is to be added to the maximum. If the funding has been greater than the accrual, a prepaid expense asset appears on the balance sheet, and the maximum is to be reduced by interest on this asset.

The minimum accrual or charge under APB 8 is essentially the normal cost under the actuarial cost method chosen, plus interest on the initial accrued liability and on any additional accrued liability resulting from later plan amendment, plus an adjustment for vested benefits, plus or minus an adjustment for actuarial gain or loss. APB 8 raises the minimum accrual somewhat above the "normal cost plus interest" concept (but never higher than normal cost plus level amortization over 40 years) if the unfunded present value of already vested benefits does not diminish by at least 5 percent of itself each year. The minimum, like the maximum, is to be adjusted upward (or downward) by interest at the valuation rate on any balance sheet liability (or asset) arising from the past accruals being different from past funding.

Left to the actuary is the choice of an actuarial cost method, including the method of adjustment for actuarial gain or loss, and the choice of actuarial assumptions. APB 8 endorses all of the usual actuarial cost methods, except for terminal funding. Presumably without-supplemental-liability methods are considered satisfactory, despite the range of acceptable accruals being stated in with-supplemental-liability terms. APB 8 shows a preference for spreading the actuarial gain or loss in a systematic manner, and for valuing common stocks on a market value basis.

The direct effect of APB *Opinion No. 8* on the security of pension expectations was minimal, because it imposes no conditions whatsoever on the funding of the employer's pension plan. The minimum cost accrual provisions can be met by setting up a balance sheet liability on the employer's books, in lieu of a contribution into a trust fund outside the employer's control. Balance sheet reserve plans, common in the early days of pensions, really offer little additional measure of security to employees, because the reserve item is not irrevocably committed to the payment of pension benefits.

There may well have been, however, an indirect effect of the issuance of APB 8, favorable to employee benefit security. This opinion applied to current disbursement or pay-as-you-go plans as well as to those operating on advance funding principles, and had the effect of encouraging a shift from the former to the latter. If an employer is required by APB 8 to charge his operating statement with at least the required minimum, there is little incentive to fund less than this amount, especially since he can get a tax deduction only to the extent that the accrual is funded.

Accrual of pension costs on a basis different from the funding is complicated and confusing, and not at all natural to the average employer. It is likely that the accrual of pension costs is synonymous with the funding thereof in the great majority of private pension plans.

Since the minimum requirement under APB 8 is higher than any requirement under the IRS rules, the accounting rule may have effectively increased the level of funding slightly. Perhaps an even greater effect is that APB 8 clearly discourages erratic accrual of pension costs, and indirectly discourages erratic funding as well. Clearly it imposes a discipline on employer funding, and takes away some of the flexibility that employers had before APB 8 was issued.

It is perhaps a bit surprising that APB 8 makes one bow to employee benefit expectations. It recommends that the amount of any unfunded present value of vested pension benefits be shown among the footnotes. This is a far cry from treating such unfunded amount as a true liability—but it does warn an employee who reads the fine print of his or her employer's financial statement if all vested benefits are not completely funded.

It is worth noting here the reason why the unfunded present value of vested benefits is presented in financial statements only as a footnote, and not as a liability. A great majority of pension plans include a specific statement that the employer established the pension plan with the express understanding that the liability of the employer in connection with the pension plan is no greater than the assets already contributed. The relatively few employers who voluntarily assume legal liability for some or all of the benefits earned to date are likely to have pension assets greater than these liabilities.

APB *Opinion No. 8* also recognizes that an employer may have voluntarily assumed a liability beyond the amount of his funding, even though this has not been common practice. If this is the situation, APB 8 recommends the setting up of the unfunded amount of the liability assumed as a balance sheet liability, but also suggests an offsetting asset. It is not clear to the authors what the effect of these compensating entries really is, but they consider it of no real consequence in view of the relative rareness of the practice. It will be seen later that APB 8 is likely to be modified in view of the 1974 legislation, and this seeming anomaly may well be cleared up.

THE EMPLOYEE RETIREMENT INCOME SECURITY ACT OF 1974

The federal legislation signed into law in September 1974 will have a major impact on the regulatory environment within which private pension plans operate. As the title of this act implies, its main thrust is toward the security of employee pension expectations, one of the major goals of pension funding.

Several of the ERISA provisions, important though they may be, do not have an important effect on the problem to which this work is addressed. The new requirements as to eligibility and vesting affect the design and the scope of the pension plan. The new fiduciary requirements affect the conduct of certain persons associated with the plan. ERISA provisions in these categories are largely extraneous to the pension funding problem, and will not be further discussed.

The new minimum funding requirements, the requirements on the newly established "enrolled actuary," and certain implications of the guarantee of pension benefits by the Pension Benefit Guaranty Corporation, are in a different category. These will have an important and immediate effect on the pension funding problem. In many ways it is too early to assess the full impact of ERISA, since many of the regulations interpreting its very complex provisions have yet to be issued. It nonetheless appears that at least the following provisions will have an impact.

Minimum Funding Requirements

1. The minimum funding requirements have been strengthened. The purpose of these requirements is to enhance employee security in pension expectations, and to lower the potential for claims against the Pension Benefit Guaranty Corporation. The minimum funding requirement is stated accumulatively. Funding equal to the normal cost, plus an amortization of the accrued liability by level payments over a fixed period of years, is required. The periods of years for minimum amortization, different for single versus multiple employer plans and for plans already in existence versus newly established plans, are as follows:

   a. Thirty years for the initial accrued liability of newly established single employer plans, and for any additional accrued liability resulting from future amendment to single employer plans.

   b. Forty years for the unfunded accrued liability of new or existing multiple employer plans, for any additional accrued liability resulting from future amendment to multiple employer plans, and for the existing unfunded accrued liability of single employer plans already in effect when these provisions of ERISA become effective.

2. Amortization of unfunded accrued liability changes resulting from actuarial gain or loss is to be over a 15-year period for single employer plans, 20 years for multiple employer. However, for purposes of determining the minimum level of funding, actuarial gain or loss can be spread in the same fashion as the present value of future normal costs if the actuarial cost method is one of the aggregate or frozen initial liability methods.

3. The minimum funding requirements apply to nearly all defined-benefit pension plans in the private sector. Current disbursement or pay-as-you-go plans are effectively outlawed, except for governmental employers to whom ERISA does not apply, and except for some specifically stated situations of relatively minor importance.

4. There are special provisions for

   a. Extending the amortization periods in special circumstances where the regular rules can be shown to be onerous.

   b. Spreading the effect of changes in actuarial assumptions or actuarial cost methods.

   c. Keeping track of where the funding stands with respect to the minimum by means of a "funding standard account."

5. The law includes an alternate minimum funding standard, the purpose of which is to make possible the abandonment of the continued amortization of the entry-age accrued liability, once the accrued liability under the accrued benefit cost method has been fully funded. There also seem to be provisions, dealing with later unfunding due to depreciation of plan assets, that may discourage the use of this alternate.

Maximum Funding Provisions

6. The maximum deductible employer contribution has been raised. A *ten-year* spread of the initial accrued liability (and of any additions thereto arising from plan amendment) substitutes for the 10 percent spread in the pre-1974 Internal

Revenue Code. However, the former "5 percent of covered payroll" choice has been eliminated.

7. The maximum deductible employer contribution is reduced when the unfunded accrued liability becomes zero, to the level of the normal cost. Should the assets exceed the accrued liability, the maximum deductible employer contribution is further reduced to adjust for the "overfunding."

The Enrolled Actuary and his Responsibilities

8. The Secretaries of Labor and Treasury are directed to establish a class of persons to be known as "enrolled actuaries." The requirements to be met before an actuary can be enrolled involve both education and experience, but the details are left largely to regulation.

9. Each defined-benefit pension plan in the private sector must engage an enrolled actuary, who is then responsible for certifying that the plan meets the minimum funding requirements. The law views the enrolled actuary as acting in behalf of the plan participants rather than the plan sponsor, although it is often the latter who will pay the actuary for his or her services. It is possible that, under some circumstances, the enrolled actuary may be considered a fiduciary.

10. Certain restrictions or limitations are placed on the enrolled actuary's methods, or upon the assumptions chosen.

    a. The actuary is expected to use assumptions that in the aggregate represent a "best estimate" of anticipated experience.

    b. The valuation of common stocks, making up a part of plan assets, must be based in some way upon market values. Averaging techniques reflecting market values over the past appear to be permitted.

    c. It appears that he or she must use a single actuarial cost method and a single set of assumptions for all plan purposes; although this interpretation comes from the committee reports rather than from the law itself.

    d. Although the enrolled actuary can choose his or her own actuarial cost method, accrued benefit, entry-age normal, aggregate, individual level premium, attained age normal and frozen initial liability are specifically recognized. These names may differ slightly from the terminology employed in this book, but correspond to the descriptions in Chapters 5 through 8.

Guarantees on Plan Termination

11. ERISA provides mandatory plan termination insurance, operating through a federally sponsored Pension Benefit Guaranty Corporation, for insured accrued benefits. Only benefits vested under the terms of the plan are insured. There is a limit beyond which benefits for any one individual are not insured. Vested benefits created by changes in plan provisions within five years prior to plan termination are only partially insured.

12. A contingent employer liability is created, through a provision by which the Pension Benefit Guaranty Corporation has a legal claim against the employer, in an amount up to 30 percent of the employer's net worth, if the Pension Benefit Guaranty Corporation is called upon to make good on its guarantee with respect to insured benefits for employees. This contingent liability did not exist before the passage of the 1974 legislation, and under ERISA it may be possible to discharge the contingent liability by purchase of insurance. Its effect on the employer's financial statement is yet to be determined. Presumably APB *Opinion No. 8* will be revised in the light of ERISA, and the handling of this contingent liability is one of the matters that the accounting profession has under consideration.

17

Actuarial Reports

No MATTER HOW good an actuary's performance may be in selecting and applying an actuarial cost method, in choosing actuarial assumptions, in adjusting for experience gain or loss, and in carrying out the calculations, his job is not complete until he has communicated his results and recommendations to those particularly concerned.

There is no standardized format for displaying results of actuarial valuations of pension plans, but there is substantial help in the Guides to Professional Conduct of the American Academy of Actuaries, the Conference of Actuaries in Public Practice, and the Society of Actuaries, and in the Opinions that interpret these Guides. Opinions A–4, C–4 and S–4 of the Academy, the Conference, and the Society respectively all include the following:

> In the furnishing of reliable information the actuary is typically in a position of rendering advice based on the interaction of many assumptions, some of which are not susceptible of accurate statistical prediction. Therefore, the actuary has a responsibility to avoid misunderstanding by means of adequate disclosures. Accordingly, in the opinion of the Committee the actuary's report, in addition to including the name of the actuary directing the report and his professional affiliation, should consider the following elements and give sufficient detail, where pertinent, to permit an objective appraisal of the valuation by another qualified actuary.
>
> a. The name of the person or firm retaining the actuary for the report, and the purpose which the report is intended to serve.
> b. An outline or reference to an accessible outline of the plan of benefits being valued.

  c. The effective date of the valuation, the date as of which the
      data were compiled, sources of data and any assumptions
      made with respect to unavailable census information.
  d. A summary of the statistics pertaining to the group, broken
      down according to significant categories such as retired, active
      and terminated-vested, together with the book and market
      values of assets and the asset value used in the valuation.
  e. A summary of the basic valuation results with a suitable state-
      ment relative to an appropriate level of pension cost and an
      appropriate range in contributions.
  f. A statement of the actuarial assumptions and methods, includ-
      ing, where appropriate, an appraisal of their suitability for the
      purposes at hand and reference to factors which have not been
      considered. Changes in actuarial assumptions from those used
      in previous reports should be stated and their effect noted.
          This statement should not be limited to factors explicitly
      assumed but should include a reference to the handling or
      absence of consideration, of such other factors as the actuary in
      his judgment deems to have pertinence in an evaluation of
      future costs or cost incidence in terms of the purpose to be
      served by his report. Such factors, for example, may include in-
      flation, probable margins, effect of plant shutdowns, etc.

Despite the lack of standardization in pension actuarial reports,
inclusion of certain kinds of information, in addition to that suggested in the above quoted opinion, seems to be indicated. (24)
ERISA requires certain information from the enrolled actuary
serving the plan, particularly a showing as to the meeting of minimum funding requirements. An employer subject to income tax
will need a demonstration that his contribution is deductible. A calculation of the unfunded present value of vested pension benefits
may be needed for the employer's financial statement.

A checklist of information that might be considered for inclusion
in a report of an actuarial valuation of a defined-benefit pension plan
appears below. Some of the items do not apply to all kinds of plans,
and others need be included only when there is special interest.

  1. Statement of actuarial cost method employed, including means
      of adjustment for actuarial gain or loss.
  2. Statement of actuarial assumptions, accompanied by whatever
      justification is felt to be desirable, and any qualification that
      the actuary feels necessary.

3. Summary of data on which the valuation is based, and an indication of its date and source.

4. A summary of pension fund assets by type, including the methods of valuing each type of asset, and a calculation of the asset values.

5. Normal cost, and its employer and employee portions.

6. Accrued liability, and its unfunded portion.

7. Maximum deductible contribution.

8. Calculation of the "funding standard account" required by ERISA.

9. Present value of accrued benefits, and the portion applicable to vested benefits.

10. Recommendation as to the magnitude of the employer contribution for the ensuing period.

11. Actuarial statement and signature required of the enrolled actuary by ERISA.

A full-blown analysis of actuarial gain and loss is not often necessary, but the actuary will want to satisfy himself as to the more important sources of such gain or loss, and may wish to include a statement of his conclusions.

Some actuaries may wish to include a statement of income to and disbursements from the pension fund, tracing thereby the change in the level of pension assets. A display of the changes in employee census data since the last valuation may be useful, particularly when changes are pronounced.

Good communications require a careful explanation of any terms that may be unfamiliar to those to whom the report is addressed.

appendix

The Illustrations

THE ILLUSTRATIONS throughout this volume are based on a hypothetical population of active workers changing over time; and a hypothetical pension plan providing benefits to retirees.

A. THE POPULATIONS

1. Mortality and employee withdrawal rates are assumed to be in accordance with the service table illustrated on page 140. Since all hiring is assumed to be at age 30, and all workers are assumed to retire upon attainment of age 65, the service table is for ages 30–65 only.

   a. Death rates are approximately those of the 1971 Group Annuity Mortality Table representative of male mortality.

   b. The average x of the l_x column in the table is 40.6.

   c. Ten percent of the entrants at age 30 are still in service when they reach age 65.

x	l_x	d_x	w_x	d_x/l_x	w_x/l_x
30	1,000	1	162	.00100	.16200
31	837	1	130	.00119	.15532
32	706	1	105	.00142	.14873
33	600	1	85	.00167	.14167
34	514	1	66	.00195	.12840
35	447	1	41	.00224	.09172
36	405	1	28	.00247	.06914
37	376	1	25	.00266	.06649
38	350	1	23	.00286	.06571
39	326	1	20	.00307	.06135
40	305	1	16	.00328	.05246
41	288	1	15	.00347	.05208
42	272	1	12	.00368	.04412
43	259	1	11	.00386	.04247
44	247	1	11	.00405	.04453
45	235	1	11	.00426	.04681
46	223	1	10	.00448	.04484
47	212	1	9	.00472	.04245
48	202	1	9	.00495	.04455
49	192	1	9	.00521	.04688
50	182	1	8	.00549	.04396
51	173	1	8	.00578	.04624
52	164	1	7	.00610	.04268
53	156	1	7	.00641	.04487
54	148	1	6	.00676	.04054
55	141	1	6	.00709	.04255
56	134	1	5	.00746	.03731
57	128	1	4	.00781	.03125
58	123	1	4	.00813	.03252
59	118	1	3	.00847	.02542
60	114	1	3	.00877	.02632
61	110	2	1	.01818	.00909
62	107	2	1	.01869	.00935
63	104	2		.01923	
64	102	2		.01961	

2. Mortality rates for those who have retired, and for those who have left employment with vested benefits, are assumed to be as follows. Since the earliest age at which vested benefits can exist is 40, the table starts at that age. Death rates again are approximately those of the 1971 Group Annuity Mortality Table, representative of male mortality.

x	q_x	x	q_x
40	.00328	65	.02000
45	.00426	70	.04598
50	.00549	75	.05970
55	.00709	80	.10638
60	.00877	85	.11538
		90	.18182
		95	.33333

3. An initial group of 10,000 employees, all initially hired at age 30, is assumed to be distributed by age as follows. Initially there are no retired employees or vested terminations. The firm came into existence 35 years ago, and has grown since.

x	l'_x	x	l'_x
30	1,240	50	162
31	1,042	51	154
32	875	52	146
33	735	53	137
34	617	54	128
35	519	55	119
36	441	56	110
37	379	57	101
38	330	58	92
39	290	59	82
40	261	60	72
41	240	61	60
42	226	62	47
43	217	63	31
44	208	64	16
45	200		
46	192		
47	184		
48	177		
49	170		

The average age of this initial staff is 38.6.

4. As time passes, the l'_x column above is subjected to decrement by death and withdrawal (in accordance with service table in 1) and by retirement at attainment of age 65. The growth of the employee group has ended, so that just enough hiring is done, all at age 30, to keep the active staff constant at 10,000. The staff ages for about 30 years as a result of the cessation of staff growth, then oscillates. Average age after 10, 20, 30, 40, and 50 years is as illustrated below:

Time	Average Age
0	38.6
10	40.3
20	40.7
30	40.9
40	40.5
50	40.6

5. As the process continues, the number of retirees grows. These are illustrated below:

Time	Number of Retirees
0	0
10	472
20	1,043
30	1,303
40	1,549
50	1,531

The number of those who terminated vested before age 65 also grows, and some of these attain age 65 and become retirees as well. These are not included among the retirees shown above.

6. As a last step in the calculations, the decimal point was moved one place to the left. The illustrations are therefore actually based on a population $\frac{1}{10}$ the size of that indicated in 3, 4, and 5 above.

B. THE HYPOTHETICAL PENSION PLAN

The illustrations in this book are all based on a hypothetical pension plan providing the following benefits.

1. Benefit formula—1.5 percent × years of service × average salary over the last ten years of employment. Straight life annuity form.
2. Retirement age—65.
   Early or late retirement—none.
3. 100 percent vesting after ten years of employment.
   Vested benefit, to begin at 65, in accordance with regular benefit formula applied at termination.
4. Ancillary death or disability benefits—none.
5. Employee contributions—none.

C. THE NONINFLATIONARY MODEL

1. It is assumed that employees have been and will be hired at $6,000 per annum; and have salary increases of 1.5 percent per year, all attributable to experience or promotion. The rate of pay just before retirement is $9,954 per annum, and the ten-year final average is $9,317.
2. The initial payroll is $6,883 per worker. As the population ages the payroll increases slowly, reaching $7,138 per worker after 30 years. Thereafter it oscillates, approaching the limit of $7,099 per worker.
3. The assumed investment earnings rate is 4 percent.

D. THE INFLATIONARY MODEL

Illustrations for Chapter 13 are based on an inflationary model, different from the noninflationary model of C in the following respects:

1. In addition to the 1.5 percent salary increase for the promotional effect, a general salary increase of 5 percent per calendar year is assumed. Starting salaries also increase at 5 percent.
2. Total payroll therefore increases 5 percent per year faster than noninflationary model, reaching $17,949 per employee in the 20th year, $77,471 in the 50th.
3. Benefits after retirement increase at 3 percent, in recognition of consumer price increases of that amount.
4. Investment earnings rate—7 percent for Tables 2A through 9A; 9 percent for Tables 2B through 9B

In summary, compared to the noninflationary model, the inflationary model has the following changes in the inflation related assumptions:

	As to Salary Increase	As to Investment Earnings	As to Benefits after Retirement
Tables A...............	+5%	+3%	+3%
Tables B...............	+5%	+5%	+3%

Pension Funding Terms

The following is a list of pension funding terms appearing in the text. For each entry the page where the term is first introduced is indicated. Terms used by other authors, but which are not a part of the terminology adopted for this volume, are indicated by an asterisk.

Following the list of terms is an indication of the terminology and classification scheme for the actuarial cost methods discussed.

Term and Page Number

Classification of Actuarial Cost Methods—with Page References

Aggregate Cost Methods
  Original Form, 55
  Entry-Age Form, 57
  Accrued Benefit Form, 60

Frozen Initial Liability Methods
  Entry-Age Form, 64
  Accrued Benefit Form, 65
  Attained Age Normal, 65

Other Actuarial Cost Methods
  Individual Level Premium, 68
  Terminal Cost Method, 22

List of References

Reference Number	Author	Title
1	Adams, W. R.	"The Effect of Interest on Pension Contributions." *Transactions of the Society of Actuaries,* no. 19 (1967), pp. 170–83.
2	Allison, G. D., and Winklevoss, H. E.	"The Interrelationships among Inflation Rates, Salary Rates, Interest Rates, and Pension Costs." *Transactions of the Society of Actuaries,* no. 27 (1975).
3	Anderson, A. W.	"A New Look at Gain and Loss Analysis." *Transactions of the Society of Actuaries,* no. 23 (1971), pp. 7–47.
4	Arnold, E. A.	"Inflation and Retirement Plans." *Proceedings of the Conference of Actuaries in Public Practice,* no. 20 (1971), pp. 56–85.
5	Bassett, P. C.	"Accounting for Pension-Plan Costs on Corporate Financial Statements." *Transactions of the Society of Actuaries,* no. 16 (1964), pp. 318–34.

Reference Number	Author	Title
6	Berin, B. N.	*The Fundamentals of Pension Mathematics.* Chicago: Society of Actuaries, 1972.
7	Bowers, N. L., Hickman, J. C., and Nesbitt, C. J.	"Introduction to the Dynamics of Pension Funding."—To be published in *Transactions of the Society of Actuaries,* (1976).
8	Bronson, D. C.	"Pensions—1949." *Transactions of the Society of Actuaries,* no. 1 (1949), pp. 219–55.
9	Bronson, D. C.	*Concepts of Actuarial Soundness in Pension Plans.* Homewood, Ill.: Richard D. Irwin, Inc., 1957.
10	Cooper, S. L., and Hickman, J. C.	"A Family of Accrued Benefit Actuarial Cost Methods." *Transactions of the Society of Actuaries,* no. 19 (1967), pp. 53–59.
11	Cowen, J. L.	"The 1962 RRB Mortality and Remarriage Tables." *Transactions of the Society of Actuaries,* no. 17 (1965), pp. 58–73.
12	Crocker, T. F., Sarason, H. M., and Straight, B. W.	*The Actuary's Pension Handbook.* Los Angeles: Pension Publications, 1955.
13	Dreher, W. A.	"Gain and Loss Analysis for Pension Fund Valuations." *Transactions of the Society of Actuaries,* no. 11 (1960), pp. 588–635.
14	Dreher, W. A.	"Alternatives Available Under APB Opinion No. 8; An Actuary's View" *Journal of Accountancy,* (September 1967), pp. 37–51.
15	Fellers, W. W., and Jackson, P. H.	"Non-Insured Pensioner Mortality— The Up-1984 Table." To be published in *Proceedings of the Conference of Actuaries in Public Practice,* no. 25 (1976).

Reference Number	Author	Title
16	Fleischer, D. R.	"The Forecast Valuation Method for Pension Plans." To be published in *Transactions of the Society of Actuaries* (1976).
17	Francis, P. R., and Scholey, J. K.	"Pension Fund Finance— Equalisation of Burdens and Accumulation of Assets." *Transactions of the 18th International Congress of Actuaries*, no. 1 (1968), pp. 651–60.
18	Griffin, F. L., Jr.	"Concepts of Adequacy in Pension Plan Funding." *Transactions of the Society of Actuaries*, no. 18 (1966), pp. 46–65.
19	Griffin, F. L., Jr., and Trowbridge, C. L.	*Status of Funding Under Private Pension Plans.* Homewood, Ill.: Richard D. Irwin, Inc., 1969.
20	Hamilton, J. A., and Jackson, P. H.	"The Valuation of Pension Fund Assets." *Transactions of the Society of Actuaries*, no. 20 (1968), pp. 386–417.
21	Hanson, J.	"What is the Added Cost to Permit Unrestricted Election of Optional Forms of Retirement Income?" *Transactions of the Society of Actuaries*, no. 13 (1961), pp. 169–80.
22	Hanson, J.	"Precision in Pension Funding." *Proceedings of the Conference of Actuaries in Public Practice*, no. 16 (1967), pp. 329–47.
23	Hazlehurst, B. H.	"Significance of Choice in Approach to Certain Actuarial Assumptions." *Proceedings of the Conference of Actuaries in Public Practice*, no. 19 (1970), pp. 109–24.

Reference Number	*Author*	*Title*
24	Hazlehurst, B. H.	"What Should Be the Content of a Soundly Conceived Actuarial Report?" *Proceedings of the Conference of Actuaries in Public Practice,* no. 21 (1972), pp. 138–46.
25	Hickman, J. C., and Montgomery, D. B.	"Pension Funding Under Wage and Price Inflation." *Actuarial Research Clearing House,* Society of Actuaries, no. 3 (1975).
26	Hicks, E. L.	*Accounting for the Cost of Pension Plans.* New York: American Institute of Certified Public Accountants, 1965.
27	Hicks, E. L., and others.	*Accounting for the Cost of Pension Plans—Accounting Principles Board Opinion No. 8.* New York: American Institute of Certified Public Accountants, 1966.
28	Marples, W. F.	"Salary Scales." *Transactions of the Society of Actuaries,* no. 14 (1962), pp. 1–30.
29	Marples, W. F.	*Actuarial Aspects of Pension Security.* Homewood, Ill.: Richard D. Irwin, Inc., 1965.
30	Marples, W. F.	"Cost of Vesting in Pensions." *Transactions of the Society of Actuaries,* no. 18 (1966), pp. 277–95.
31	McGill, D. M.	*Fundamentals of Private Pensions.* 3d ed. Homewood, Ill.: Richard D. Irwin, Inc., 1975.
32	McGill, D. M.	*Fulfilling Pension Expectations.* Homewood, Ill.: Richard D. Irwin, Inc., 1962.

Reference Number	Author	Title
33	McGill, D. M.	*Preservation of Pension Benefit Rights.* Homewood, Ill.: Richard D. Irwin, Inc., 1971.
34	McGill, D. M., and Winklevoss, H. E.	"A Quantitative Analysis of Actuarial Cost Methods for Pension Plans." *Proceedings of the Conference of Actuaries in Public Practice,* no. 23 (1973), pp. 212–43.
35	McGinn, D. F.	"Indices to the Cost of Vested Pension Benefits." *Transactions of the Society of Actuaries,* no. 18 (1966), pp. 187–242.
36	Melone, J. J.	"Actuarial Cost Methods—New Pension Terminology." *Journal of Insurance,* no. 30 (1963).
37	Sarason, H. M.	*Advanced Pension Tables.* St. Louis: Insurance and Pension Press, Inc., 1974.
38	Shannon, A. G., Jr.	"Valuing Liberal Early Retirement Benefits—Problems and Practical Solutions." *Proceedings of the Conference of Actuaries in Public Practice,* no. 21 (1972), pp. 75–86.
39	Shur, W.	"Financing the Federal Retirement Systems." *Transactions of the Society of Actuaries,* no. 16 (1964), pp. 265–93.
40	Taylor, J. R.	"A Generalized Family of Aggregate Actuarial Cost Methods for Pension Funding." *Transactions of the Society of Actuaries,* no. 19 (1967), pp. 1–12.
41	Trowbridge, C. L.	"Fundamentals of Pension Funding." *Transactions of the Society of Actuaries,* no. 4 (1952), pp. 17–43.

Reference Number	Author	Title
42	Trowbridge, C. L.	"The Unfunded Present Value Family of Pension Funding Methods." *Transactions of the Society of Actuaries,* no. 15 (1963), pp. 151–69.
43	Trowbridge, C. L.	"ABC's of Pension Funding." *Harvard Business Review,* (March–April 1966).
44	Trowbridge, C. L.	"Cost of Vesting in Private Pension Plans." *Transactions of the Society of Actuaries,* no. 24 (1972), pp. 397–410.
45	Walker, D. A.	"A Staff Pension Fund." *Transactions of the Actuarial Society of America,* no. 16 (1915), pp. 109–44.
46	Winklevoss, H. E., and Shapiro, A. F.	"Estimating the Cost of Vesting in Pension Plans." *Transactions of the Society of Actuaries,* no. 24 (1972), pp. 373–94.
47	U.S. Treasury Department, Internal Revenue Service	*Bulletin* on Sections 23(p)(1)(A) and (B), 1939 Internal Revenue Code, 1945.